LIFE SKILLS FOR TEENAGE BOYS

A STRAIGHTFORWARD GUIDE TO SMART MONEY MANAGEMENT, SOLID CONFIDENCE, HEALTHY LIVING, AND RELATIONSHIP UNDERSTANDING FOR THE BEST TEEN YEARS A BOY CAN HAVE

Bright Futures Publications

TABLE OF CONTENTS

I'm so glad that you have chosen to purchase this book, as a gift for you reading this book below is a QR code which you can scan to gain access to our free worksheet ebook which is needed to follow the challenges in this book and, you'll gain exclusive access to new books when they come out!

Introduction

Welcome to the roller-coaster ride called teenagerhood—where every day brings something new, fun, and sometimes scary. Maybe you're stepping into the halls of high school for the first time or getting ready to spread your wings and fly into the adult world.

Let's face it: Being a teenager can feel like trying to solve a Rubik's Cube blindfolded. One minute, you're feeling on top of the world, acing that math test or scoring the winning goal. The next minute, you're questioning your entire existence, wondering if you'll ever figure out what you want to do with your life.

Growing up can be confusing. Everything is changing, but at the same time, you have a lot to learn and a lot to do. Sometimes, it might feel as if you can't keep up. When you become a teenager, your brain and body start changing, and how you think about yourself will also change.

A world of grownup activities and responsibilities is ahead of you, but you're not quite there yet.

When you're growing up, it often feels like there's no rule book for navigating the ups and downs of teenage life. You're faced with countless choices, challenges, and uncertainties, and it can sometimes feel like you're flying blind.

That's why we decided to write this book as a road map to surviving and thriving during your teenage years. It's packed with valuable insights and practical advice to help you tackle everything from building independence and managing your time to developing resilience and making tough decisions.

It's a practical, no-nonsense guide to help you not only survive but also thrive during these exhilarating yet crazy years.

This book will help you level up your game, from boosting your confidence and mastering the art of small talk to figuring out how to stretch your allowance and even make your own money.

Keep in mind, though, that it's *not* only about acquiring skills but also about *embracing* the journey and becoming the best version of yourself along the way. So, get ready for the journey of a lifetime.

We want to encourage you to make this book truly your own. Highlight the passages that are meaningful to you, make notes, and process the information in any way that is meaningful to you.

CHAPTER 1:

SELF-DISCOVERY: WHO AM I?

Becoming a teenager could feel like someone is playing a prank on you. Your body is changing and doing weird things when you least expect it.

As Jake stepped into his teenage years, it felt like someone had pressed the start button on a game he wasn't prepared to play. His body began to change in ways that left him feeling like a character in a game he didn't quite understand.

A dedicated gamer, Jake could see the similarities between his virtual adventures and the real-life transformations he was experiencing. Like his favorite characters leveling up, his physical appearance seemed to evolve overnight. His face started looking different; he had unexpected voice cracks and unwelcome acne.

Whenever he thought he had a handle on things, he experienced a new challenge. His voice betrayed him at inconvenient moments, leaving him feeling as though he was in a game that was glitching.

Emotionally, he felt as if he was on a roller-coaster ride, with peaks of confidence followed by valleys of uncertainty.

He felt unstoppable on some days, and on others, he felt uncertain about himself.

Jake also discovered that many of his gaming friends were experiencing similar transformations, and it became easier to deal with all the changes as they supported each other through the journey they were experiencing.

Throughout this book you may feel like Jake and you may feel overwhelmed however this book is there to help you, and to guide you onto the path of adulthood.

Changes to Your Body

Like Jake, you may start noticing changes to your body as you get older. You're getting bigger, your voice changes, and you also start getting body hair amongst other things. These changes are also known as puberty, and they happen to most boys between the ages of 9 and 14 - don't worry if you don't fall into this age bracket though. Puberty can be late in some teens, it gets the nickname "late bloomers". Being a late bloomer is NOTHING to be worried or ashamed about, it is normal and you WILL catch up to your friends who may have already started puberty before you.

Bodies change at a different pace, so you and your friends or siblings may not experience all the changes in the same way and at the same time. Genetics will also play a role in your body's development; for example, you could grow as tall as either of your parents or even end up somewhere between them. Enough exercise and a healthy diet will also influence how your body develops and even when you develop muscles, which many boys want to know more about.

You'll have to be patient when it comes to developing muscles, as there is no way to rush the process, but taking part in weightlifting once you start puberty can contribute to your muscle development.

Growing body hair as a teenager is also a natural part of life. You may suddenly find hair on your face, chest, armpits, and pubic hair. Don't worry about it too much in the beginning. Later, you could ask your dad, or whoever else you want, for some shaving tips.

You will probably become sweatier (and smellier) due to hormone changes. As long as you shower regularly and use deodorant, you'll be okay.

Erections are another interesting development of puberty and have to do with more blood flowing to your private part. They can happen when you're sleeping or when you are awake, having an erection is nothing to be ashamed about - it is normal. You may develop sexual feelings and feel the need to touch yourself or masturbate. It's normal to want to explore your body as the hormones inside you are changing how you feel. You just need to make sure you do this in a private place.

Some of your friends may talk about the crushes they have on people, but it's also normal if you haven't developed romantic feelings for anyone yet. Your hormones could be causing confusing emotions and thoughts during this hectic time. As you grow older and meet new people, you may find that they don't follow "traditional" rules (which is okay) and they may like the same gender as they are. You must remember to respect people who choose to make that decision as it is theirs to make and not yours.

Another interesting surprise is that your voice can be squeaky at times and then gradually get deeper. This is because your larynx, or voice box, is getting larger. You'll also see that you develop an Adam's apple at the front of your neck.

You could experience some unfortunate skin changes, such as pimples and acne on your face, neck, back, shoulders, and chest. Don't get too depressed about this, as these are temporary changes caused by hormones and in general, keeping a good skincare routine will keep most acne at bay.

Changes to Your Mind

When you become a teenager, a lot of changes will also happen in your brain. You'll have to deal with all kinds of academic, social, and emotional challenges while your brain is still developing.

This is a long and ongoing process, and some parts of your brain, such as the ones that regulate your mood, help you pay attention, and think abstractly, might only reach maturity by the time you're 25.

Some parts of your brain will mature earlier than others, and the imbalance can cause you to be moody and impulsive.

There are things you can do to make sure you make the best decisions, such as slowing down and thinking things through. Think about *why* you want to act in a certain way, and never feel rushed to make decisions, especially if they could have serious consequences.

Plan your future and get excited about it. You're less likely to make poor decisions now if you have goals and plans. Have a vision for your life after high school. It also makes it easier to get through uncertainties if you know better days are ahead.

If you're struggling with certain things, such as sleeping, eating, exercise, or your social life, ask your parents for advice. If you think you're developing a health problem, it's usually better to get to a doctor as soon as you can, but never feel too ashamed to speak to someone who cares for you about how you are feeling.

If you're struggling socially, be patient with yourself. The part of your brain that interprets the emotions expressed by others is still developing, and you can misread social cues, which could make it a bit more difficult to manage your friendships and relationships. If you offend someone unintentionally, apologize and learn from your mistakes.

Development Differences

Becoming a teenager is different for everyone. Hormones change your body and neural pathways, influencing how your brain learns and develops. While you may find something easy to learn, puberty could make it difficult for your friend to learn the same thing.

Speaking of hormones, we haven't even explained what they are. Hormones like testosterone and estradiol affect your brain and various other organs. In the brain, testosterone influences your medial amygdala, which likely contributes to gender-based differences in the brain. They also cause changes to your body, such as hair growth and muscle development.

How soon you experience puberty can be dependent on your genes and experiences during early childhood. If you experienced stress in your early childhood, you could enter puberty sooner than others. But this isn't something to worry about if you start puberty early or late, as for everyone puberty will happen.

Hormones not only influence the structure of your brain but also determine how it responds in certain environments and situations. All of these hormonal changes can affect certain cognitive functions (this is just a fancy way of saying brain activity). For example, all the changes happening in your body can affect how your brain processes memory, attention span and overall brain function. This could explain why it's difficult to learn new skills whilst going through puberty.

However, there are other important types of learning that take place when you're a teenager; you'll develop greater self-awareness and build more social skills. You're also more likely to want to explore and take risks.

BECOMING CONFIDENT

Confidence is about believing in yourself and your abilities. You don't have to be the loudest or most outgoing person in the room; you just have to be cool with who you are. Appreciate your uniqueness, and don't try to change yourself to fit in with others. It's about believing that you can do things, whether it's passing an exam or asking someone out who you've admired for a while.

An important part of confidence is accepting yourself for who you are, including your appearance. Don't worry if you struggle to appreciate yourself sometimes, as these feelings are also normal.

Self-esteem and confidence go hand in hand. Self-esteem is almost like your personal rating system; it's about how much you like and value yourself. You feel good about yourself when your self-esteem is high; it's almost like having a positive mindset about yourself.

Think of self-esteem as the overall vibe you have about yourself. It's like your personal rating system—how much you like and value yourself. When your self-esteem is high, it's like you're giving yourself a big thumbs up. You feel good about who you are, believe in what you can do, and don't let mistakes bring you down.

Peer Pressure

When you were younger, your parents probably chose most of your friends, but now that you're growing up, you're going to want to choose your own friends. You'll likely end up spending more time with them than your family.

As a teenager, you can become more social, and friends can play an important role in your life. Your friends and classmates may try to influence you to act in certain ways or do certain things, and that's when you'll start to experience peer pressure. You'll influence each other in a variety of ways.

It's normal to want to be with your peers and to want to fit in with them. However, you must remain authentic and not change yourself for other people.

Teenagers learn from each other, and your peers can have a positive influence on you. You can learn from each other and inspire each other. However, if they have a negative influence on you and you cave to peer pressure, you may end up doing the wrong thing.

Some kids who are desperate to fit in could succumb to peer pressure. When you have strong self-confidence and know what's right and wrong, you'll be less likely to succumb to peer pressure. If you have a friend who stands by you, it's even easier to stand up to peer pressure.

It's entirely possible to plan for peer pressure situations by doing things like surrounding yourself with like-minded friends or just being able to say no without feeling that you have to explain yourself. If you feel a situation is getting out of control, always ask your parents or other adults for support.

MINDFULNESS

Mindfulness is about being fully present and engaged in the current moment without being distracted or judging your own thoughts. It involves paying deliberate attention to your thoughts, feelings, and sensations.

Mindfulness can benefit you in the following ways:

- It can boost your concentration, helping you nail those study sessions that will improve your grades.
- It provides you with the tools to handle stress and master your emotions. Mindfulness is a great way to prevent yourself from being overwhelmed by that roller coaster of emotions.
- Mindfulness is your personal guide to understanding your thoughts, feelings, and who you really are.
- It helps you build your social skills and build stronger connections with others.
- If you're an athlete, it will help you sharpen your focus, manage stress, and kick your skills up a notch.

- Mindfulness lets you pause before making that life-changing decision.
- If you struggle with sleep, mindfulness has your back with relaxation tricks and mindful breathing.
- Mindfulness can even help you beat peer pressure, live an authentic life, and make choices that matter to you.
- Life is full of ups and downs. Mindfulness teaches you to bounce back stronger from setbacks.

When you're trying out mindfulness, keep in mind that you might not find it that easy to begin with. Getting the hang of mindfulness skills can be a bit tricky initially, so cut yourself some slack and give it time. Take note of the little victories as the exercises start feeling less daunting.

As you stick with the practice of mindfulness, you might notice it's easier to focus on things such as schoolwork or really listening to others. It's like unlocking a sense of calm and patience in your day-to-day life. Dealing with the little annoyances of daily life might also become a little bit easier.

Mindfulness Exercise

Try this mindful breathing exercise:

1. Sit or lie down in a comfortable decision and place a hand on your chest and one on your stomach.
2. Close your eyes and relax your muscles, starting with your toes. Work your way up. Pay attention to releasing the tension in your face, neck, and jaw.
3. Take slow, deep breaths for a few minutes and make your stomach rise and fall rather than just your chest.
4. Focus on each breath. Concentrate on inhaling and exhaling, visualizing the tension leaving your body every time you exhale.
5. Be aware of any wandering thoughts, and gently bring your focus back to your breath. Picture your distracting thoughts drifting away like balloons.

Key Takeaways

- Puberty brings physical changes such as growth spurts, voice changes, body hair growth, and hormonal fluctuations.
- Exercise, diet, and genetics influence development, including muscle growth and hair patterns.

- Body changes such as erections, sweating, and acne are normal during puberty.
- Teenage brain development involves emotional, social, and cognitive changes.
- Developing self-awareness, decision-making skills, and coping strategies are essential during adolescence.
- The onset of puberty varies due to genetics and early life experiences.
- Hormonal changes influence brain structure and cognitive functions, impacting learning and behavior.
- Confidence involves self-acceptance, belief in one's abilities, and resilience.
- Self-esteem plays a crucial role in confidence, influencing self-perception and mindset.
- Strategies to deal with peer pressure include surrounding oneself with supportive friends and seeking adult guidance.
- Mindfulness involves being present, non-judgmental, and attentive to thoughts and feelings.
- Benefits of mindfulness include improved concentration, stress management, self-awareness, and decision-making.

In Chapter 2, we're going to look at time management and how you can use it to shape your life for the better.

Chapter 2:

Time Management and Productivity

Time is a precious resource that shapes our lives. If we know how to manage our time, we can achieve more in life and be more productive. Time management is especially important for a busy teenager who has to balance the demands of school, a social life, and responsibilities at home.

Time Management

Time is the currency of life, and as a teenager, luckily, you still have a lot of it available. Learning how to manage your time can change your life for the better.

When you started middle school, your life changed quite a bit. You now have more homework, the school work is more difficult, and even your extracurricular activities have become more demanding.

Your schedule at school might have become more complex. Where you probably had a single teacher before in your familiar classroom, now you might have different teachers and classrooms, classes in different buildings, and you can hardly keep up with your schedule. This can be a scary time because everyone wants you to take more responsibility while you feel like having fun and spending time with your friends.

Don't feel bad if you're struggling to stay on top of things. As we learned in the previous chapter, your brain development might be holding you back. There is a link between time management and how your brain is developing, as you'll experience rapid brain growth when you enter middle school and move from concrete to abstract thinking.

While time management isn't easy, there are things you can do to keep track of your life. Write everything down, create visible reminders, peer support groups, and decide your own priorities are great ways to start. Write your important dates down on a calendar and break your long-term goals into smaller milestones.

Time Management Tips

One practical way of getting through the early morning rush is to prep your bag the night before.

Here are some other useful tips for preparing the night before school:

- Take a glance at your schedule for the next day. Note which classes, subjects, and any extracurricular activities are on the agenda.
- Collect all the necessary textbooks, notebooks, and any assignment or project materials related to the scheduled classes. Make sure you have all the right tools for the job, including pens, pencils, and any specialized equipment.
- If pending homework or assignments are due the next day, make sure they are completed and neatly tucked into your bag. This prevents the last-minute scramble in the morning and will reduce your stress levels.
- Don't forget items such as a water bottle, lunch, and any relevant permission slips or forms. Having these essentials packed and ready reduces the chances of forgetting important things.
- Give your bag a once-over to make sure you have packed everything you need. This includes ensuring your device, if needed, is charged and ready for use.

GOAL SETTING

Goal setting is an important skill you need to get ahead in life. It gives you a sense of purpose, and if you have goals, you'll be motivated to make something of your life. Without goals you may feel like your life is stuck in one direction, or that life may be a little boring. Creating goals that get you excited is a key factor in having a fulfilling life.

Mapping Your Week Ahead

Mapping your week ahead allows you to visualize your time and allocate it efficiently to ensure you're progressing toward your goals. For example if you know you have 5 days of school but you want to practice sports, a new language or anything - you'll need to map your week ahead to create time for this practice.

You can start by asking yourself what you accomplished during the last week and what you hope to do during the current one.

Scan the QR code at the front of this book and you'll find a daily planner that you can use to put what you have just learnt into practice! Don't be afraid to use it just once, use it as many times as you want.

SMART Goals

Have you heard of SMART goals? It may sound complicated, but it's simply a goal-setting framework. Each letter in the name refers to criteria that define and achieve objectives.

- Specific: Clearly define the goal. Be precise about what you want to achieve, as vague goals can only confuse you. For example, if you want to improve your grades, specify by how much and when.
- Measurable: How will you check if you were successful? With the example of your grades, it's fairly simple.
- Attainable: Set goals you know you will be able to achieve. It shouldn't be too easy to achieve, but you will only be frustrated if the goal is completely out of your reach; for example, if you set the goal of achieving an A for math, your worst subject. It might be a more attainable goal to achieve a C.
- Relevant: Align your goal with your broader objectives and aspirations. It should be meaningful and contribute to your overall growth and development. For example if you need an A in math for college then that is contributing to your wider objective. Or you could do extra practice at a sport you love, this could then boost your chances of making that sport more than just a hobby.

- Time-Bound: Set a specific timeframe for achieving the goal. A deadline creates a sense of urgency; for example, you need to improve your mark for math by the end of the term.

Why Are SMART Goals Important for Teenagers?

SMART goals are important for the following reasons:

- They give you a clear understanding of what you want to achieve. They will help you use your time and efforts for a specific outcome.
- They make it easier to see how far you've come, and you can adjust your goals or celebrate your achievements.
- They help you break your goals down into smaller steps that are easier to manage. They teach you time management, organizational, and problem-solving skills.
- They build your confidence when you achieve your goals and help you feel a sense of accomplishment.
- They help you gain a sense of responsibility.

Short-Term vs. Long-Term Goals

Short-term goals are like the little victories you aim for in your day-to-day life. They are the stuff you can get done fairly quickly; for example, if you have an English assignment you need to submit on Friday, you can write a little bit every day until it's done by the due date.

Long-term goals are like your big dreams, and they usually take more time and effort; for example, if you decide your ultimate aim is to get an A in English by the end of the term. This won't happen overnight, but you can set your short-term goals toward achieving it; for example, by submitting all your assignments and working on them every day. This way, your short-term goals will add up to your long-term goals.

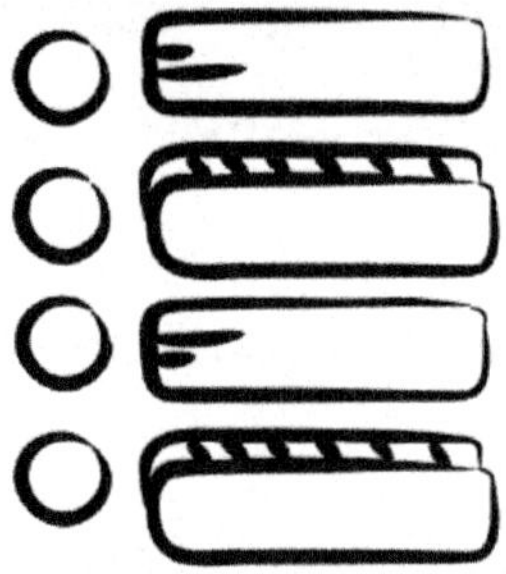

Prioritization

You've got a ton of stuff going on: homework, projects, hanging out with friends, maybe even a part-time job. Prioritizing is like having a road map that guides you through all of it, making sure you tackle the important stuff first - but most importantly, leaving you with plenty of time to enjoy what makes you happy.

You can practice your prioritization skills on the homework you have to do every day. First of all, make a list of what you have to do for every subject. What needs to be done for the next day? This should be higher on your priority list. Give your tasks a rating from 1 to 5 based on their importance. Figure out how much time each task will need and plan your finish and start times.

What's in It for You?

- Prioritization helps you figure out what is the most important and what you need to do first. It can help you get your homework and other tasks done quicker.
- You don't need to rush to get things done and can do them better. For example, if you're going to a camp with your friends, you can prioritize what to plan and buy for the camp. If you do a little bit every day, you shouldn't have to do so much the day before you go.
- If you prioritize, you'll be able to handle things better, such as keeping your school stuff together.
- You'll be able to manage your time better, and you won't miss out on those special times with your friends, such as a barbecue or movie night.

Let's look at some examples of how you can prioritize the balancing act that's your life.

The Weekend Warrior

Imagine it's the weekend, and you've got a bunch of things you want to do: hang out with friends, binge-watch a series, and participate in an online gaming tournament. However, you also have a school project that you have been putting off and is now due next week.

Is your mind spinning and you don't know where to start? Instead of just diving into one thing, you need to prioritize. Do your school project first and reward yourself with breaks to do the other stuff; for example, you can visit your friends for an hour and then come back to work on your project again, or you can watch an episode of your series before continuing with your work.

Adapting to Change

Your teenage years can be like a physical, emotional, and social roller-coaster ride through an ever-evolving world.

One day, you might be happy and make new friends, while the next might be full of storm clouds, conflicts, and challenges. Teenage life can be unpredictable, but it's also when you can create lifelong memories.

There is always going to be some form of change in your life, but there are ways you can learn to deal with it. The world is unpredictable, and we won't always be able to control what happens to us. However, we can control how we *react* to what happens to us.

It can be difficult to deal with change, as we mostly prefer what is familiar to us. Change can cause discomfort or be hard work, but it often leads to personal growth, and we become better people.

Some people resist change, but this isn't a good long-term strategy. After a while, you could find it more uncomfortable to stay the same than having to change. If you refuse your change, you can limit your growth, and you will eventually feel stuck.

Refusing to change means you can miss out on opportunities and relationships.

How to Adapt to Change

When major changes happen in your life, take some time to process them. If others pressure you to make decisions, tell them you need time to think about things. If you experience unpleasant feelings, take some time to think about them and let them go.

Work on changing your negative thoughts about something, as it's also a way of accepting what's out of your control. For example, if your girlfriend ends her relationship with you, reflect on your good times together, but admit to yourself that you didn't fit that well together, and it's healthier for you to move on.

Change can be positive; for example, it's very exciting to finish your time at school and start studying at a prestigious university.

When change is difficult or uncertain, it can negatively impact your mood and energy; for example, if your parents divorced and you now have to travel between two different households. In times like these, you need to take it easy on yourself.

If the changes in your life feel overwhelming, speak to an adult or a mental health professional about them.

Healthy Breaks and Relaxation

Let's talk about the power of taking a breather and looking after your mental well-being. Life can get pretty hectic with school, sports, and all the other stuff you have to juggle. That's why you need to take a break now and again.

Your brain is almost like a computer working on tons of tasks at once. Sometimes, it needs a break to cool down and perform at its best.

Stepping back for only a short while can make a big difference. Go for a short walk with your dog, play video games, or even just listen to a few of your favorite songs. This gives your brain the fuel it needs.

Let's look at some relaxation techniques:

- When you get stressed, take a deep breath. Close your eyes, inhale, and hold your breath for a few moments. Then, exhale and repeat this exercise until you feel your tension going away.
- Progressive muscle relaxation is a cool trick you can use to relax your muscles. Tense up one muscle group at a time for a few seconds, then release them. Maybe start with your fists or shoulders.

- Guided meditation or simple mindfulness exercises can also help you relax. Chat with your friends or family when things get rough; everyone needs their own support squad.

Key Takeaways

- Time is valuable, especially for teenagers balancing school, social life, and responsibilities.
- Managing time involves writing everything down, creating visible reminders, seeking peer support, and setting priorities.
- SMART goals (specific, measurable, attainable, relevant, time-bound) aid in setting clear and achievable objectives.
- Prioritizing tasks helps manage time effectively and ensures important activities are addressed first.
- Relaxation techniques include deep breathing, progressive muscle relaxation, guided meditation, and mindfulness exercises.
- Seeking support from friends and family helps manage stress and build resilience.

In Chapter 3, we will look at the money skills that will help you get ahead in life.

CHAPTER 3:

MONEY SKILLS 101

Have you always wished you could get your hands on a lot of money to buy whatever you want? If your parents or other adults have significant debt, they will probably advise caution. They will tell you to be careful and save or invest your money.

It's important to start building a healthy relationship with money at a young age, so that you are equipped with essential money skills into your adult life.

INTRODUCTION TO MONEY

Let's break down the concept of money in a way that connects with your daily life. Imagine money as a scorecard for the time, effort, and resources you've put into various activities.

Now, let's talk about the equation: Money = Time + Effort + Resources.

Time

Think about time as the hours you spend on different tasks—studying, working, playing video games, or enjoying yourself with your friends. Each moment contributes to your overall "time score."

Effort

This is the energy and hard work you put into everything you do. Whether it's studying for a test, practicing a sport, or helping out at home, your effort adds up to your "effort score."

Resources

Resources can be anything from money itself to the skills you acquire, the knowledge you gain, and even the connections you build. All these things are like tools in your tool kit that help you get through life.

When you combine your time, effort, and resources, you get your total "money score." Money is a tangible representation of all the things you invest in.

As you enter adulthood, money becomes a tool that helps you turn your dreams into reality. Want that cool gaming setup? Saving money is like converting your time and effort into the gear you desire. Dreaming of traveling the world? Your resource score—the skills and knowledge you gain—can help you make it happen. Your skills will help you get a job that will pay for your travels, and you could even work your way around the world if you have certain skills, for example, if you're an English teacher.

Understanding this equation empowers you to make wise choices. It's not just about having cash in your pocket; it's about valuing your time, appreciating your hard work, and using your skills to create a better future for yourself. So, in the years ahead, mastering this game of life, where money is the score, becomes crucial. It's not just about earning money; it's about making the most of your time, effort, and resources to create a fulfilling and successful journey.

Making Your Own Money

Do you get an allowance but also want to start making your own money? There's nothing like earning your own cash to boost your self-esteem. This is where a part-time job or side hustle comes in handy. What makes this even more of an exciting challenge is that because of technological development, you can make money through multiple income streams. Gone are the days when making extra money meant getting a job at a fast-food restaurant. You can now run multiple side hustles at the same time.

So, what is a side hustle? It's a part-time job or gig you can do alongside your main activities, like school. It's a way to earn extra money, gain independence, explore your interests, and learn valuable skills. This could be anything from selling items online, tutoring another student, or working as a server. It can be anything as long as it's something you enjoy doing and fits your schedule.

Multiple Side Hustles

Side hustles, especially multiple side hustles, can be a stepping stone to future opportunities and success. Just imagine that by the time you leave school, you can already have a successful business running.

Multiple income streams can also boost your finances in an unstable economy. Think of it this way: If you lose one job or customer, you'll still have others providing you with an income.

Building various income streams will also contribute to your future financial freedom. Remember, it's not just about how much money you can make but also the freedom to decide how you want to spend your time. The days when you had to spend 30 years working the same 9-to-5 are long gone. Many more options are available to lead a meaningful life and build a career that matters to you.

Here are some examples of cool things you can do to earn cash. There are many options available online, which means you don't even have to leave your house, which might be a safer option when you're still at school and will also be less likely to disrupt your studies.

- You can work as an online tutor. This could involve helping others master a school subject you're a whiz at. Math tutors are often in high demand. You could also tutor children at your school in the classroom or library if that space is available. Many people still prefer in-person tutors.
- If you're a master of the English language and have patience, the world of English teaching is open to you. There is a huge demand for English teachers worldwide, both online and in person. If you teach online, you can manage your classes to fit in with your schoolwork. Some of these jobs require a degree, but many are available that don't, and some only require you to have conversations with the students.
- You can make money from a YouTube channel or podcast through ads, sponsorships, or affiliate marketing. After all, wealthy YouTuber Mr. Beast started his channel when he was 14 years old. Today, at 25 years old, he is worth millions of dollars.
- You could even make money by writing a book or creating art to sell online. There have been some

surprisingly young people who have been successful at doing this.

- You could sell your handmade arts and crafts online.
- If you're a fitness freak, you could do wellness coaching or even become a personal trainer in your free time. Everything you do doesn't have to be online, you need to find a way that will work for you.
- Serving at a restaurant or working in a shop might seem old-fashioned now, but this can teach you very useful things, such as how to work with people and customers, which can come in handy in your future career.

Looking for a Job

Have you decided to look for a part-time job? You should know a few things about crafting your resume and doing job interviews.

Crafting Your Resume

Writing a strong resume is like putting your best foot forward on paper. This could sound like a scary process if you haven't done it before, but it's quite simple.

1. Start with your contact info: your name, phone number, and email. These must be easy to find, as people may want to contact you for an interview.

2. Next, write a short objective or summary about what you're looking for in a job. List your skills, focusing on those that match the job you want. Before you apply for a job, you should make sure that it at least matches most of your skills.
3. When it comes to work experience, go from the most recent job to the oldest, detailing your role and responsibilities. If you don't have experience, focus on the extracurricular activities you do at school.
4. Showcase any achievements or projects you're proud of. If you've done volunteer work, include it. This shows you're involved in the community and proactive.
5. Keep the formatting simple and easy to read, using bullet points and a clean font.
6. Customize your resume for each job application and emphasize the skills and experiences the employer is seeking. You'll probably also have to provide a cover letter with your application, which you should keep as short and simple as possible.
7. Proofread your resume to catch any typos or mistakes—a polished resume reflects your attention to detail.

Your resume is your personal marketing tool. Keep it clear, truthful, and focused on why you're the perfect fit for the job. You can also browse the internet for examples and templates of resumes and cover letters.

The Interview

Preparing for a job interview is about showcasing your best self. You need to search for information about the company you are applying to and understand exactly what they do. You'll make a good impression if you appear knowledgeable during your interview.

Familiarize yourself with your resume and be ready to talk about your experience and skills. Anticipate common questions, such as strengths and weaknesses, and practice your responses.

You should also dress appropriately and arrive on time for the interview. Pay attention to body language, smile, and maintain eye contact. Make sure you listen carefully to the questions before answering.

When introducing yourself to the interviewer, emphasize your experience and suitability for the job. When discussing strengths and weaknesses, focus on those relevant to the position and indicate that you're willing to learn and improve. Try to be as authentic and confident during your interview as possible.

Advice on Common Interview Questions

Interviewers usually have some common interview questions. You can prepare for them as follows:

- Tell Me About Yourself

This is usually an icebreaker, and you should focus on your professional life. Briefly mention your education and relevant experiences and highlight your skills that align with the job.

- What Are Your Strengths and Weaknesses?

This question can be difficult, as you don't want to say something that will prevent you from getting the job. Strengths are the easy part of the question, and you should focus on qualities relevant to the job. Try to frame weaknesses in a positive way and show that you're committed to improving. For example, you could say that you tend to be critical of your work but that this is encouraging you to continually improve.

- Why Do You Want to Work for This Company?

Your answer should reflect your admiration for the company's values, culture, and achievements. This is also why you should do enough research before the interview.

Budgeting Basics

Budgeting is the key to making your money work for you. If you know the basics, it will help you down the road.

Even if you don't have a regular income as a teen, budgeting helps you make the most of the money you earn or receive as an allowance. It's not just about saving for that laptop or game you want; it's about building good habits for the long run.

Budgeting 50-30-20 Rule

This simple rule helps you allocate your income effectively:

- 50% for needs: Essentials such as food, shelter, and clothing fall under this category.
- 30% for wants: This is for things you desire but aren't necessities, such as video games, gadgets, or non-essential clothing.
- 20% for savings: Save a portion for future goals or unexpected expenses.

We'll get into more details about this system a little later.

The Jar System

Are you wondering how to set up a budget when you've just started your first job and haven't received that much money yet? Keep things simple. You can use a jar system and label jars or envelopes with categories such as saving, spending, or sharing.

When you get your money, allocate some to each jar; this will help you see where your money is going and spend more responsibly.

Needs vs. Wants

Before you decide how to spend your money on your needs and wants, you need to understand the difference between them. Needs are items you need to survive, such as food and clothes. Wants are things you would like to have, but they aren't really necessary, for example, the latest gaming console or that cool pair of designer shoes.

When you're putting your budget together, you first have to look at your needs before you put money aside for things you want but don't really need.

Budgeting Tips

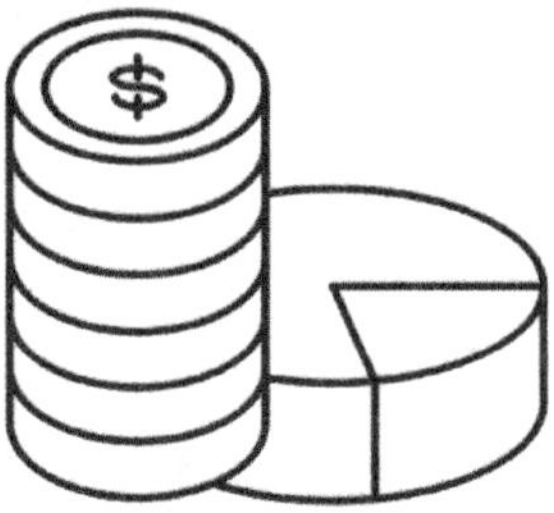

A basic budget is simple, although you might find it daunting before you begin. Start by adding up all the income you get in a month. Next, you need to know what you spend, and you can start with regular expenses such as subscriptions or memberships. Once you know how much of your income you spend, you can set aside the money you want to save or spend.

When you know your income and expenses, you can set up your budget. Once you have a budget, you have to be disciplined and stick to it. A budget can help you with your self-control and lay the groundwork for financial success.

Make sure you regularly review your budget to align with your changing needs and priorities.

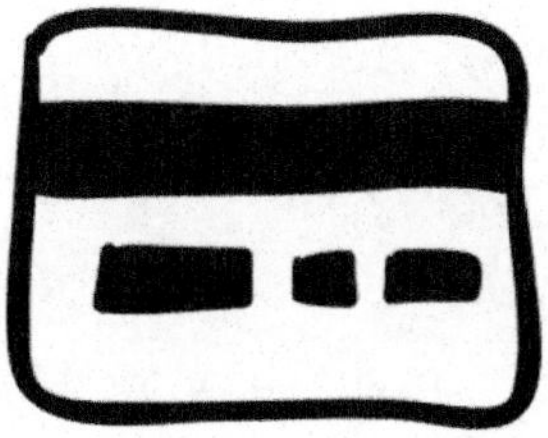

DEBT AWARENESS AND EMERGENCY FUNDS

It can be tricky to manage your money, and things can go wrong quickly if you aren't careful. You could be spending all your money on the fun times you have with your friends, just enjoying your life, and then your phone decides to bite the dust, or your motorcycle needs some serious repairs. What do you do then? Are you feeling stuck and stressed out?

For times like these, you need an emergency fund or some cash you've put aside that can save the day. A solid emergency fund is your ticket to financial freedom. Let's look at how you can deal with debt and still set aside some money to deal with debt.

Dealing With Debt

Debt—it's a short but scary word. Maybe you've heard your parents complain about it. If you haven't got any debt, keep it that way for as long as possible.

Debt is when you owe money to someone or someplace because you borrowed it. It's like borrowing a game or a book from a friend and promising to return it later. However, when you borrow money, you have to pay it back with some extra, which is called interest. If you borrow money, you have to make sure you can pay it all back in time so you don't end up in a difficult financial situation. You'll create debt when you spend beyond your means.

Be careful of credit card debt, as many stores and businesses will be eager to offer you one. You also usually have to pay high interest on your credit card.

There is good debt and bad debt. Buying those shoes you don't need on your credit card is an example of bad debt. Good debt is money you use to service your long-term goals that will improve your life, such as paying for your education and starting your own business.

Emergency Fund

As you get older, you'll realize how important it is to plan for unexpected things happening in life, including from a financial perspective.

An emergency fund is money you set aside for these unforeseen expenses; for example, if you lose your phone and it's up to you to replace it.

It's a great idea to keep your emergency fund aside from your other savings, as it's for emergencies only. This isn't money you're going to use for parties or a new wardrobe. However, you should be able to access this money easily when you need it in an emergency.

You could be wondering how much money you should have in your emergency fund, but it is hard to give a straightforward answer to this question. No one can predict what kind of emergency you'll have to deal with and how much it will cost. If you've put some money aside, you already have a head start. Try to aim for at least a few hundred dollars, or enough to cover 3-6 months of any expenses you have leaving your account each month.

Savings and Goals

When you start saving your money, you need to have some practical goals in mind. First off, let's take another look at the 50-30-20 rule so we're all on the same page:

- 50% of needs go toward the essentials—stuff like food, bills, and keeping a roof over your head. These are the things you can't live without.

- 30% is for wants or the enjoyable things you treat yourself with, such as going out with your friends and buying that pair of shoes you really need.
- 20% is for your savings or money for your future needs. This money will help you build your financial future.

You need to have some goals for your savings. We've already talked about the emergency fund or that few hundred dollars you need to stash away for whatever unexpected expenses might come your way.

You may also want to save for that dream purchase, such as a trip with your friends. If you're saving for your dream, set a target amount and put money away until you can make it happen.

Maybe you want to go to college, and you know that your parents won't be able to support you financially. By starting to put away money for your education now, you can contribute to making your college dream possible.

Do you have a side hustle and already have quite a bit of money you want to put away? Think about investing some of it in bonds, stocks, and mutual funds. There is some risk involved, so make sure to research before you do anything. You could also ask an adult for advice.

Remember, saving your money isn't all just about being responsible; it's also about enjoying your life.

The 100 Envelope Challenge

Are you ready for a fun and rewarding savings challenge?

The 100 Envelope Challenge is a cool way of saving money by stashing away a bit every day. You can start with a small amount, like 10 cents, and work your way up to $10.

Here's how it works:

1. Take 100 envelopes—or you can use jars and containers if that's more your style.
2. Label your envelopes with different amounts. You can start at 10 cents and increase it by 10 cents each time. So, you'll have envelopes labeled 10 cents, 20 cents, 30 cents, and so on, all the way up to $10.
3. Every day, or whenever you can, pick an envelope and put that amount of money inside. It might not feel like much at first, but it will add up fast.
4. Keep going until you've filled all 100 envelopes. By the time you reach the end, you could have saved a few hundred dollars.

This technique will help you save a chunk of money, and you'll also learn some valuable money skills.

1¢ 365 Challenge

If you don't have a regular income yet, this challenge is for you. The 1¢ 365 Challenge is all about saving one cent a day for an entire year. It sounds small, but it will add up. We've even got a handy template for you to track your progress.

Scan the QR code at the start of the book to get access to our templates just for this book!

After completing this challenge, you'll understand the power of setting goals and saving up for something specific.

Whether it's a trip with friends or a future investment, setting goals gives your money a purpose and motivates you to stick to your savings plan.

Pay the Right Price

Let's talk about a super important skill: comparison shopping. You know how sometimes you see something you want to buy, but before you hand over your hard-earned cash, you want to make sure you're getting the best deal? There's no worse feeling than paying a lot of money for something and then seeing it somewhere else for half price.

That's where comparison shopping comes in.

Prices can vary a lot, depending on where you buy something. For example, your favorite chocolate might be cheaper at the store down the street. The book you've been waiting for might also be cheaper online than at your local bookstore.

You can help your parents with grocery shopping to get the hang of comparison shopping. Pay attention to the prices of different items at different shops. This will help you understand the value of money and make smart spending decisions.

Taxes and Credit (for the Future)

You've probably heard adults talk about taxes, but do you know what it's all about? You'll only really have to worry about it once you're an adult, but it's good to start learning about it now so you can still get a comprehensive understanding of how finance works.

What Are Taxes?

Taxes are mandatory fees individuals and businesses have to pay to the government. These fees are used to fund projects and services that benefit everyone in the community; for example, books for public libraries will be paid from tax money.

This is income tax, capital gains tax, property tax, and sales tax. Each one is applied differently and goes toward different things.

Who Pays Taxes?

People and companies must pay taxes on their income, profits, sales, and property holdings above a certain threshold. It's mandatory, and there are penalties for those who try to dodge their tax responsibilities.

Why do we pay taxes, and where does the money go? Taxes help fund parks, playgrounds, hospitals, and other services. The money goes to different levels of government.

For example, property taxes go to local governments, while income taxes go to federal and state governments.

Local taxes might go toward building schools and parks, while federal taxes might fund things like Social Security and defense.

Taxes are paid yearly, and sales taxes are usually paid at the time of purchase.

You can ask one of your parents to show you their paycheck and explain how taxes impact your take-home pay. This could also help you understand why it's important to budget.

Mini Activity: Practice Saving Receipts

Try out this activity—saving receipts. Even if you're not paying taxes yet, this is a great habit to develop for the future.

Here's what you can do:

1. Grab a small box or envelope to store your receipts. You can even decorate it to make it your own!
2. Decide on a goal for saving your receipts. Maybe you want to see how many you can collect in a month or aim to save receipts from specific types of purchases.
3. Whenever you buy something, ask for a receipt and put it in your designated box or envelope.

4. Keep track of how many receipts you've collected and watch your collection grow over time. You can even create a chart or graph to visualize your progress.
5. At the end of the month, take some time to think about your receipt-saving journey. Did you meet your goal? What did you learn?
6. For an extra challenge, try categorizing your receipts by type of purchase (e.g., food, entertainment, school supplies) or by amount spent. This can help you see where your money is going and identify areas where you might be able to save more.

KEY TAKEAWAYS

- Money represents the time, effort, and resources invested in various activities.
- Budgeting helps make money work for you.
- The 50-30-20 rule allocates income: 50% for needs, 30% for wants, and 20% for savings.
- Needs are essential for survival (e.g., food, shelter), while wants are desires (e.g., video games, designer shoes).
- Debt should be avoided if possible, as it involves paying back borrowed money with interest.

- An emergency fund is essential for unexpected expenses and financial security.
- Comparison shopping helps make informed spending decisions by finding the best deals.
- You can practice comparison shopping by assisting with grocery shopping and noting price variations.
- Taxes are mandatory fees paid to the government to fund public projects and services.
- Different types of taxes include income tax, capital gains tax, property tax, and sales tax.
- Taxes help finance parks, hospitals, schools, and other essential services.

In Chapter 4, we will consider why it's so important to learn good communication skills as a teenager.

CHAPTER 4:

COMMUNICATION IS KEY

Many people think communication is about talking as much as possible, but this isn't the case. It also has a lot to do with listening. You need to be able to sit back and listen to what someone else has to say.

Being able to interpret other people's body language is also important because you need to be able to decode those nods, shrugs, and eye rolls. These actions often speak louder than the words people use.

Communication can also help you get through those conflict situations. There will always be times when things get heated, especially if you have a few hot-heated friends together.

In those cases, instead of getting physical, you need to talk it out. You'd be surprised how far staying calm and talking about things can take you.

Online communication can be an entirely different ball game when it comes to communication. It's easier to misunderstand someone if you can't see their expression or hear their tone of voice. That's why thinking twice before you hit send is important.

Verbal vs. Nonverbal Communication Skills

One of the first things you need to do when working on your communication skills is to improve your listening skills. Don't zone out when someone's talking to you; show them you're actively listening to them by nodding and asking questions.

Your body language should also show that you're listening to the conversation. Stand up straight and make eye contact. Eye contact tells someone you're paying attention and that you respect them. Speak in a friendly tone and get to the point before people lose interest.

You can also use hand gestures to punctuate your speech. If you're one of those people who talk with your hands, they can emphasize your message or even clarify its meaning.

Practice controlling your facial expressions, as they can tell others what you're thinking and how you're feeling at that moment. Also, learn to read others' facial expressions.

Tips for Confident Speaking

Verbal communication can help you forge connections and make your voice heard. However, clear and confident speaking takes practice. So, level up your verbal communication skills and command the attention of any room.

Projecting Your Voice

Have you ever felt as if your words get lost in the wind? Turn up the volume and make sure your message is heard loud and clear. Here's how:

- Stand tall and breathe deeply from your diaphragm.
- Speak from your chest, not your throat, and imagine your voice filling the room.
- Practice speaking with energy and enthusiasm to project your voice naturally.

Speaking at a Steady Pace

It can be challenging to find the right pace of speaking. Here's how to strike the perfect balance:

- Aim for a steady rhythm, like a smooth jazz beat.
- Pay attention to your audience's reactions. If they look confused, you might be speaking too fast or you may be mumbling - slow down and speak clearly
- Practice speaking slowly and deliberately, especially when conveying essential points.

Removing the "Fluff"

Ums, ahs, and other verbal fillers can sneak into your speech like unwelcome guests at a party. Here's how to get rid of them:

- Pause instead of using fillers; it gives you time to gather your thoughts and emphasizes your words.
- Record yourself speaking and listen for patterns of filler words.
- Practice speaking without filler words, focusing on clarity and precision.

Dealing With Conflict

You'll always have to deal with conflict in life, and you're already one step ahead if you know how to deal with it. If you become involved in an argument, there are certain things you can do to prevent it from escalating and becoming physical.

Here are five easy steps you can follow to stop any fight:

- Step back from a disagreement and calm down. The more angry things you say to each other, the more likely your argument or fight with someone is to escalate. If you keep insulting each other, you're more likely to get angrier.
- When there's a problem, you need to communicate clearly and discuss what you want the outcome to be.

- Everyone who is involved in the situation should brainstorm solutions.
- Select a solution that will work for everyone involved in the situation.
- Even when disagreeing with someone, you should still value their opinions.

Remember that to resolve conflicts effectively, you should avoid negative behavior such as refusing to listen to others, name-calling, or violence.

More Conflict Resolution Tips

Here are more useful tips that can help you deal with conflict:

- People have different personalities and various ways of dealing with conflict. You get the "bulldozer," the guy who steamrolls over everyone; the "doormat," who lets others walk all over him; and the "doormat with spikes," sneaky and passive-aggressive. Then, there's the "pillar," assertive, respectful, and standing tall. Aim to be the pillar.
- Conflict can stir up a storm of emotions. It's okay if you're frustrated, sad, angry, or hurt. Take some time to understand what is bothering you and why. If you understand your feelings, you can speak your mind more clearly.

- Think before you act and do something rash. Think about what you will say or do and whether it will help or make things worse.
- Use "I" statements to take responsibility. Instead of pointing fingers, own up to how you feel. Say stuff like, "I feel upset when..."
- Conflict is a two-way street, and you should take the time to listen to others. Ask them questions and try to find common ground.
- Try to see things from someone else's point of view. Take a moment to see things from their perspective. It's important to show empathy.
- When you apologize for messing up, mean it. A sincere apology goes a long way. Forgive others, as holding on to grudges doesn't help anyone.
- After solving the conflict, figure out what you need to do next. Compromise and find a solution that works for everyone.
- Sometimes, you have to walk away when a relationship is doing more harm than good. Your well-being comes first, always.

Online Communication

Now that you've mastered face-to-face communication, it's time to look at the digital realm.

What you put online can have serious consequences, and it will stay out there forever. There are certain things you can do to communicate more effectively online and to make sure that people understand you.

Mind Your Tone

Maybe you're a real joker with a talent for sarcasm. Remember that jokes can be misinterpreted online, as people don't have the context of facial expressions or tone of voice for interpretation.

Your language should also be clear and straightforward so that most people can understand you. If you want to say something, but you're unsure how others might interpret it, skip it or clarify.

Think About Your Words

It's easy to say things you may regret later when you're chatting online. However, you must remember that once your words are out there, you can't get them back.

So, before you hit that send button, first think if what you're saying is respectful and appropriate. Even if someone else is being nasty to you online, don't make hurtful comments and avoid using offensive language.

Focus on Safety

It's exciting to connect with your friends on the internet, but it could also be risky. Don't share your personal information, such as your phone number and address, online or with someone you don't know. If someone makes you uncomfortable online, don't keep on speaking to them.

Be Aware of Cyberbullies

Have you or one of your friends been bullied at school? Unfortunately, you'll find these same types of characters, or cyberbullies, online. They spread negativity and love to hassle people online. Ignore or block these people. If someone keeps harassing you online, report them to adults, such as your parents or teachers.

Remember to always keep your details safe and never share your password and other login details with anyone. When you choose screen names and email addresses, select options that don't give away too much personal information about yourself.

Key Takeaways

- Communication isn't just about talking; it involves active listening and understanding non-verbal cues such as body language.
- Resolving conflicts involves clear communication, brainstorming solutions, and valuing differing opinions.

- Tips for confident speaking include projecting your voice, speaking at a steady pace, and minimizing verbal fillers.
- Remember to use "I" statements, empathize with others' perspectives, and prioritize well-being in conflict resolution.
- Practice active listening, control facial expressions, and engage in respectful dialogue to navigate conflicts effectively.
- When you communicate online, you need to be mindful of your tone, use clear language, and consider safety, including avoiding sharing personal information and dealing with cyberbullies.
- Safety online involves being cautious with personal information, avoiding hurtful comments, and reporting cyberbullying incidents.
- Keep passwords and personal details safe, choose screen names that don't reveal too much, and seek help from trusted adults if you have to deal with online harassment.

In Chapter 5, we'll look at the skills you need to do your chores and how useful it is to learn them while you're still living at home.

CHAPTER 5:

HOME SKILLS

Home maintenance, cooking basics, laundry tips, and car care... Maybe these don't sound all that interesting, but they are the foundation of your future independence. Let's face it: If you want to step out into the world alone eventually, you need to be able to look after yourself. Having these skills will not only show how capable and mature you are but will also save you a lot of money.

EATING WELL

Eating well can seem complicated since there is so much diet advice out there. You don't have to go on a complicated diet or starve yourself. The easiest way is to start eating healthier by making simple changes. Swap your bag of chips for a handful of nuts and put some veggies in your pasta. Drink enough water because staying hydrated will prepare you to face whatever comes your way. Sure, we know you like your coffee, energy drinks, and soda, but water is the way to go if you want to stay healthy. You can still have your other favorite drinks, but make sure you also drink enough water.

The trick is choosing foods you enjoy that make you feel good. Small changes, such as choosing whole grains, can make a big impact on your overall well-being. Also, create opportunities for indulging every once in a while, as this will prevent you from bingeing when you can't control your urges.

Cooking Skills

Like most of us, you probably love eating delicious food. Knowing how to deal with food and make nutritious meals is one of the most important things you need to know when you start out on your own.

Before you start cooking, you'll need some fresh food, and you also need to know how to keep food fresh.

We usually rely on the sell-by dates on packaging, but just because the date on a package has passed doesn't automatically mean it's time to throw it away. Sure, paying attention to expiration dates is a good idea, but you need to trust your instincts. If it doesn't smell good, throw it out.

Raw meat and veggies are crucial for keeping everyone healthy. When you're cooking, make sure to use separate cutting boards and utensils for raw meat and vegetables.

Cross-contamination is no joke, and it's the last thing you want when you're whipping up a meal. So, remember: meat on one board, veggies on another, and wash everything thoroughly in between.

If you have a lot of leftovers, you can freeze them. Invest in good quality freezer-safe containers, portion out your leftovers, and pop them in the freezer for later. It's a game-changer when you're too busy—or too lazy—to cook from scratch.

Meal planning can be a lifesaver. Take some time at the beginning of the week to plan out your meals. It saves you from the dreaded "What's for dinner?" dilemma and helps you stick to a budget—and you won't need to buy fast food last minute.

Last but not least, let's talk about spices. Don't be afraid to get adventurous with your seasonings. Sure, salt and pepper are great, but there's a whole world of flavors, such as cumin and paprika, out there waiting to be discovered.

Laundry

Let's tackle the world of laundry because, let's be real, nobody wants to rock a smelly shirt or crusty socks.

First of all, you need to sort your clothes. That doesn't mean simply tossing everything in the machine and hoping for the best. If you do that, you could end up with pink or other weirdly colored underwear if you didn't bother to sort properly.

Separate your whites, darks, and colors. Whites go with whites, darks with darks, and colors with colors. This practice helps prevent colors from bleeding onto each other and keeps your clothes looking fresh and vibrant.

When it comes to washing your clothes, temperature matters. Hot water is great for killing germs and getting out tough stains, but it can also cause colors to fade and fabrics to shrink. Cold water is gentler on your clothes and better for preserving colors and preventing shrinkage. Unless your clothes are seriously dirty or stained, choose cold water to keep them looking their best.

Next, you need to choose the right detergent. Make sure to use one that is suitable for your washing machine and clothes. Use as little as possible, as you don't need to drown your clothes in detergent to get them clean.

If you have a dryer, simply toss your clothes in, add a dryer sheet for extra freshness, and you're good to go. If you don't own a dryer, you can still hang your clothes up to dry. Grab some hangers, a clothesline, or even a shower rod, and hang your clothes up to air dry.

Once your clothes are clean and dry, don't forget to fold or hang them up right away. Trust me, nobody likes digging through a pile of wrinkled clothes to find something to wear.

Laundry might not be the most exciting task, but mastering these basics will keep you looking and smelling fresh.

CLEANING

Cleaning doesn't sound like much fun, but it's one of those things you need to learn to do to live independently.

When it comes to cleaning, using the right chemicals for the job is vital. Bleach is one of the most important ingredients in your cleaning package. It's great for killing germs and taking out stains, but it's also super strong.

Dilute it properly and never mix it with other cleaners, especially ammonia, because that can create toxic fumes. Another thing about bleach: It can stain clothes faster than you can say, "Oops!" So, be careful when you're using it around your favorite T-shirts. Once something has been damaged by bleach, there is simply no way to fix it.

When you're dealing with chemicals, always read the labels and follow the instructions carefully. Wear gloves and protective eyewear if necessary, and make sure the area you're cleaning is well-ventilated.

Cleaning can feel overwhelming, especially when you're staring down a mountain of dirty dishes or a floor that hasn't been vacuumed in weeks. It's much easier to tackle cleaning a little bit at a time. Instead of waiting until your room or house looks like a tornado hit it, try to establish a cleaning routine. Spend a few minutes each day tidying up and doing small tasks, and your space should stay clean without all the stress.

Maintenance

As you grow older, you'll find that being handy around the house is not only impressive but also incredibly practical. Whether you're living with family or in your own place, knowing some basic maintenance tasks will save you time and money and maybe even earn you some brownie points and boost your allowance.

While you don't have to be Tim the "Toolman" Taylor from your dad's favorite TV show, *Home Improvement,* there are certain skills all of us should have, even if only because it will make our lives easier. Don't worry if you don't know all of these yet; just try to learn more as you go along.

Painting

Painting is a skill that comes in handy when you want to freshen up a room or give it a new look.

Here's what you'll need:

- paintbrushes and rollers
- painter's tape
- drop cloths
- primer and paint
- stir sticks and paint trays

Start by prepping the walls, taping off edges, and laying down drop cloths. Apply primer if necessary, then paint with smooth, even strokes. When you finish, clean up after yourself.

Drilling Holes in Walls

Whether you're hanging up shelves or mounting a TV, knowing how to drill holes in walls is essential.

Here's what you'll need:

- drill
- drill bits
- wall anchors (if necessary)
- screws
- level

Use a level to ensure your holes are straight and even before you drill. If you're unsure, always ask for help.

Mowing the Lawn

Mowing your lawn can be fun and rewarding when you do it right. If you helped out Dad at home, you probably already know what to do. Before you start, make sure that your lawnmower is in good condition and its blades are sharp. Also, clear the lawn of any debris or obstacles.

The cutting height of your mower must be adjusted based on your grass type and the season. Cut off no more than one-third of the grass height at once.

Begin mowing in a straight line along the perimeter of your lawn, overlapping each pass slightly to ensure full coverage. For larger lawns, consider mowing in a pattern, like back and forth or in concentric circles. When you navigate the turns, lift the mower slightly to avoid creating uneven patches.

Cleaning Gutters

Clogged gutters can lead to water damage and pests, so keeping them clean is important. Here's what you'll need:

- ladder
- gloves
- bucket or tarp
- scoop or gutter cleaning tool

Climb up with a ladder and remove debris from the gutters using your hands or a tool. Dispose of the debris properly and rinse out the gutters with a hose.

Cleaning the Dishwasher

A clean dishwasher means cleaner dishes! Here's how to keep it in top shape:

1. Remove and clean the filter regularly.
2. Run a cycle with vinegar to remove buildup and odors.
3. Wipe down the door seal and interior with a damp cloth.
4. Check the spray arms for clogs and clean them as needed.

Regular maintenance will extend the life of your dishwasher and ensure it performs at its best.

Unclogging a Sink

If you know what you're doing, unclogging a sink is usually not that difficult. If the trouble continues, get an adult to help you, and they can decide if you need to call a plumber. Follow these steps to try to do it yourself first:

1. Remove any visible debris from the drain, such as hair or food particles.

2. Try pouring a mixture of baking soda and vinegar down the drain and follow it up with hot water to flush away the clog.
3. If the blockage persists, a plunger may be able to do the trick. Position the plunger over the drain, make sure you've got a tight seal, and give it a few firm pumps.
4. If all else fails, a drain snake or auger can help dislodge stubborn clogs. Be patient and take your time.

Unclogging a Toilet

A clogged toilet is always unpleasant, but you can use a plunger to attack the problem:

1. Position the plunger over the drain, ensure you have a tight seal, and give it a few firm but controlled pumps.
2. If that doesn't do the trick, consider using a toilet auger. Call a responsible adult if you need help with this. The augur must be inserted into the drain and gently rotated to break up and remove the clog. Don't use excessive force, as you might damage the toilet.

Replacing a Flapper and Other Innards

Before you attempt this, watching how an adult goes about it is probably best. Don't try it on your own if you haven't done it before.

1. If the toilet is running continuously or not flushing properly, it might be time to look inside. Start by turning off the water supply to the toilet.
2. Remove the tank lid and inspect the flapper, the rubber piece covering the drain. If it's worn or damaged, replacing it is a straightforward task.
3. Disconnect the old flapper and attach the new one.
4. While you're in there, check the other components, such as the fill valve and float. If any parts appear corroded or are malfunctioning, replacing them can often solve the issue.
5. Turn the water supply back on, and your toilet should be back in working order.

Dealing With Water Leaks

Knowing how to handle water leaks can prevent costly damage to your home. Here's what you need to know:

1. Locate the main water valve in your house.
2. Turn off the water supply if you notice a leak.
3. Fix minor leaks with a plumber's tape or a pipe wrench.

4. Call a professional for major leaks or if you're unsure how to proceed.

Fixing a Leaky Faucet

A leaky faucet is annoying and can increase the utility bills for your household. If you're going to do this, get an adult to help you out the first time or watch some instruction videos on YouTube. Here are the steps to address it:

1. Start by turning off the water supply under the sink.
2. Cover the drain with a plug or rag to prevent losing small parts. Most leaks occur due to a worn-out washer, so disassemble the faucet handle using a screwdriver.
3. Before replacing the old washer with a new one, make sure it matches the size and type.
4. Put the faucet back together, and you should have a leak-free faucet.

Addressing a Ceiling Leak

You might have heard your parents panicking when they discovered water spots on the ceiling. Take action sooner than later and try to find out what's happening. Here are the steps to follow:

1. Place a bucket under the leak to catch any water droplets.

2. Check if the leak is from a plumbing issue or a leaky roof. While you're figuring out the cause, think about how you can limit the damage.

A ceiling leak can be a mystery, and it's okay to call in the professionals if you can't find the cause.

Doing some of these tasks for the first time can be difficult. When in doubt, ask one of your parents or another trusted adult for advice.

Basic Car Maintenance

Learning basic car maintenance is almost like a rite of passage into the world of driving. Maybe you got your driver's license just the other day, but soon, you might be buying your first car. Then, you'll need the knowledge and confidence to keep your vehicle in good condition.

Here are some important aspects of car maintenance you should know:

The Car Manual

It's important to know where the car manual is kept. The manual contains valuable information about the car's specifications, maintenance schedule, and troubleshooting tips. Ask your mom or dad if you can look at the car manual for their vehicle and see what you can learn from it.

Oil Check and Change

Regular oil checks are crucial for maintaining the engine's health. A valuable skill you can learn is how to check the oil level using the dipstick and understand when the oil needs to be changed based on the manufacturer's recommendations or the oil's condition.

Tire Pressure

Proper tire pressure is essential for safe driving and fuel efficiency. You need to know how to check tire pressure using a tire pressure gauge and inflate or deflate the tires as necessary to match the recommended pressure stated in the car manual or on the tire sidewall.

Washer Fluid

Keeping the windshield clean is essential for visibility while driving. Check the washer fluid level and refill it when necessary. You also need to know how to use the windshield wipers effectively to clean the windshield.

Servicing a Car

Regular servicing ensures that the car is in good working condition and helps prevent potential issues. You need to service your car regularly and schedule regular maintenance appointments with a qualified mechanic or learn to perform basic servicing tasks themselves, such as changing air filters or inspecting brake pads.

Washing a Car

Keeping the car clean not only improves its appearance but also helps protect the paint and bodywork. Make sure you use the right cleaning products and techniques when you clean your family's car to avoid damaging the paint or scratching the surface.

Your Own Car

Do you already have your own car? Congratulations! In that case, there are a few more things you need to know.

The thrill of going where you want, whenever you want, is a fantastic feeling. However, owning a car comes with responsibilities.

How to Check the Oil

1. Make sure your car is on a flat surface. This will help you get an accurate oil level reading.

2. Park your car, turn off the engine, and give it a minute or two to cool down. This helps the oil settle back into the oil pan.
3. Pop the hood of your car and find the oil dipstick—a long, usually yellow, handle labeled "Engine Oil."
4. Grab a cloth or tissue, pull out the dipstick, and wipe it clean. This will help you get an accurate reading.
5. Put the dipstick back into its tube, ensuring it's fully seated.
6. Pull out the dipstick again and examine the oil level. There are markings on the dipstick, and the oil should be between the "low" and "full" indicators. If it's below the "low" mark, you might need to add oil.
7. Look at the oil's color. Fresh oil is amber, but if it's dark and gritty, it might be time for an oil change.

Checking your oil regularly will keep your engine running smoothly. If you ever notice something strange, like low oil or strange colors, you should talk to your mechanic.

How to Pump Gas

1. Pull up to the gas pump so your car's gas tank lines up with it.
2. Switch off your car; it's important to be safe.
3. Pop open your fuel door and unscrew the gas cap if your car has one.

4. See your car's fuel type; it's usually near the gas cap. Choose the right one.
5. Go inside to prepay or pay after—whatever the gas station prefers.
6. Lift the nozzle and stick it in your car's gas tank.
7. Pick your fueling speed and squeeze the handle to start the gas flowing.
8. Hold on tight and watch the fuel level. Stop when you've paid enough or filled up.
9. Release the handle, let any drips fall, and put the nozzle back.
10. Screw on the gas cap if you have one, and shut the fuel door tightly.
11. Now, you're ready to hit the road.

Follow any rules at the station, and if you're unsure, just ask.

How to Check a Flat Tire

If you get a flat while driving by yourself, don't panic. As long as you follow the steps below, you'll be fine:

1. Pull over to a safe, flat area away from traffic. Turn on your car's hazard lights.
2. Retrieve your spare tire, jack, and lug wrench. They're usually in your trunk.

3. Use the lug wrench to slightly loosen the lug nuts, but don't remove them yet.
4. Position the jack under the car, usually near the flat tire. Pump it up until the car is off the ground.
5. Fully unscrew the lug nuts and keep them somewhere safe—you'll need them later.
6. Carefully take off the flat tire and set it aside.
7. Place the spare tire onto the wheel bolts.
8. Hand-tighten the lug nuts first, then use the wrench to fully tighten them.
9. Slowly lower your car with the jack until it's on the ground.
10. Confirm that all lug nuts are tight.
11. Put your flat tire, tools, and jack back in your trunk.
12. Head to a professional tire shop as soon as you can. Spare tires are temporary.

If you feel unsafe or unsure, call for roadside assistance.

Key Takeaways

- Mastering basic home maintenance, cooking, laundry, and cleaning is important for your future independence.
- Meal planning can help you save time and money.

- Establish a cleaning routine to manage tasks effectively.
- Ask your parents or other adults for guidance when you tackle new tasks.
- Reading the car's manual can give you valuable information about the car's specifications and maintenance schedule.
- Regularly checking and changing the oil will make sure the car's engine stays healthy.
- Proper tire pressure is important for safe driving and fuel efficiency.
- Regular servicing appointments with a mechanic can help prevent problems.
- Proper cleaning techniques and products preserve the car's appearance and protect its paint and bodywork.

In Chapter 6, we'll look at why leading a healthy lifestyle is important.

CHAPTER 6:

HEALTHY LIVING

Your journey to adulthood is all about balancing newfound freedoms with responsibility, especially when it comes to your health and well-being.

Your body will be undergoing significant changes, making it increasingly important to prioritize healthy living habits that will help you lead a long and healthy life. Positive lifestyle choices will not only give you more energy but will also help you become more resilient and stronger in all aspects of your life.

SLEEPING WELL, EATING, AND EXERCISING

As a teenager, you're like an engine revving up for a long road trip called adulthood. And just like a car needs the right fuel to run smoothly, your body also needs the right stuff.

That's where a healthy, balanced diet comes in. Think of it this way: Pizzas, chips, and sodas might taste fantastic, but they're not the right kind of fuel for your body. While they'll give you a boost, they won't keep you going for long.

Our bodies need fruits, veggies, lean proteins, and whole grains. Also, don't forget to hydrate with plenty of water—

it's like giving your body a cool drink of fuel to keep everything running smoothly.

Sleeping helps us recharge our batteries, but we often don't get enough of it. When we're asleep, our bodies are busy repairing muscles, processing everything we learned during the day, and even releasing growth hormones that help us get taller and stronger. So, let's make a pact to prioritize our health by fueling our bodies with sleep and rest. After all, you should be ready to deal with the adventures that will come your way.

Good Sleeping Tips

Life becomes difficult when we don't get enough sleep. Let's look at what you can do to sleep better:

- Try to go to bed and wake up at the same time every day, even on weekends. This helps regulate your body's internal clock and makes it easier to fall asleep and wake up naturally.
- Follow a relaxing routine before you go to bed and wind down with activities like reading, listening to music, or taking a warm bath. Avoid screens, including phones and laptops, at least an hour before bed. The blue light can mess with your body's ability to produce melatonin, the hormone that helps you sleep.
- Your bedroom should be cool, dark, and quiet. Invest in some blackout curtains to block out light and

consider using earplugs or a white-noise machine to drown out any unwanted noise.

- While you probably enjoy energy drinks and soda, they could interrupt your sleep. Limit caffeine and sugary drinks, especially in the late afternoon and at night before you go to bed.
- Get enough exercise during the day. Regular exercise can help you fall asleep faster and enjoy deeper sleep. Just try to avoid intense workouts right before bedtime, as you could find it difficult to sleep afterward.
- Don't eat heavy or spicy meals close to bedtime, as they can cause discomfort and indigestion, making it harder to fall asleep. Eat a small snack like a banana if you're still hungry before bed.
- Find healthy ways to cope with stress to help improve your sleep. Try relaxation techniques like deep breathing, meditation, or journaling to clear your mind before bedtime.
- While it can be tempting to take naps, try to limit them to 20–30 minutes and avoid napping too close to bedtime, as it can interfere with your ability to fall asleep at night.

Getting enough sleep isn't only about feeling rested; it's about giving your body and brain the time they need to recharge so you can tackle whatever the day throws at you.

Remember to use the fantastic sleep tracker you can download free of charge via the QR code at the front of the book.

Healthy Eating

Promoting healthy habits is very important, especially at a time when your body is changing so much and growing so quickly.

Eating a balanced diet with plenty of nutrients, such as protein, vitamins, and minerals, is essential to support your growth spurt, build muscle, and keep your bones strong.

What a Healthy Diet Looks Like

These are the basics of a healthy diet:

- Always drink enough water, especially when you're very active and it's hot outside.
- Eat enough nutritious foods, such as fruit and veggies. They're packed with important vitamins, minerals, and antioxidants your body needs to function properly.
- Include protein in your diet. Your body needs sufficient protein, which you get from foods such as lean meats, fish, eggs, beans, nuts, and dairy products. These types of foods will help your body build and repair itself.

- Choose whole-grain options, such as brown rice, quinoa, and whole-wheat bread, to keep you feeling full and energized.
- Be mindful of fats. Healthy fats are also an important part of your diet. Avocados, nuts, seeds, and olive oil are great sources of healthy fats that support brain health and hormone balance.

If you have a sweet tooth, you may feel the need to indulge from time to time. Don't beat yourself up about that delicious, sugary snack. Having them in moderation on special occasions such as social gatherings is perfectly okay.

After a workout, your body can recover faster if you give it some quick-digesting carbs that you usually find in sugary snacks or sports drinks.

When you know you will be indulging in something sugary, make balanced choices. Try pairing sugary snacks with healthier options to balance their effects on your energy levels. For example, have a small piece of candy with some protein or fiber to help keep you feeling satisfied.

Portion Your Protein, Vegetables, and Carbs on Your Plate

Aim to make protein about 25%–30% of your plate. Protein is essential for building and repairing muscles, so it's crucial to include it in your meals.

Here are some examples of protein-rich foods and portion sizes:

- Chicken breast or turkey: Fill about a quarter of your plate with a portion about the size of your palm.
- Fish: Aim for a serving size similar to the size of your palm.
- Lean beef or pork: Have a portion that's about the size of a deck of cards.
- Eggs: Include 2–3 whole eggs or equivalent egg whites.
- Plant-based proteins such as tofu, tempeh, or legumes: Eat about half a cup.

Vegetables should take up about 50% of your plate. They provide essential vitamins, minerals, and fiber and are low in calories. Fill the majority of your plate with a variety of colorful vegetables. Some options include:

- leafy greens like spinach, kale, or lettuce
- cruciferous vegetables such as broccoli, cauliflower, or Brussels sprouts
- bell peppers, carrots, cucumbers, tomatoes, and any other vegetables you enjoy

Carbohydrates should make up around 20%–25% of your plate. Carbs are your body's primary source of energy, so it's essential to include them in your meals. Opt for complex carbohydrates such as whole grains, which provide sustained energy and fiber.

Here's how you can portion your carbs:

- Whole grains such as brown rice, quinoa, or whole wheat pasta: Fill about a quarter of your plate.
- Starchy vegetables such as sweet potatoes or corn: Fill another quarter of your plate.
- Legumes such as beans, lentils, or chickpeas: Eat about half a cup.

These are general guidelines, and your needs could vary based on factors such as activity level, metabolism, and overall health. Listen to your body's hunger and fullness cues and adjust your portions accordingly.

Exercising

Exercise might not sound appealing when you already have a full schedule. However, it's especially important as a teenager since your body is still growing and building muscles.

Exercise helps you stay strong and healthy as you grow. It builds up your muscles and bones, boosts your endurance, and keeps your heart strong. It will also help you sleep better, which is important when you have to face those early mornings at school.

Exercise is also good for your mind, as your brain releases awesome chemicals called endorphins that will make you feel happy during and after exercise. Regular exercise can also make you sharper and better at thinking and remembering.

When exercise is a regular part of your routine, you're setting yourself up for a lifetime of healthy habits. Studies have shown that active teens are more likely to become active adults. It's an investment in your future.

You're probably wondering how much exercise you really need. There are divided opinions about this, but most seem to say from 30 minutes to 1 hour on most days of the week. This doesn't mean you need to do boring workouts or run laps around a track. You can find something you find fun. Dance, find a sport you love, or take your dog for a walk in the park. When you do something you enjoy, exercise won't feel like a chore.

An exercise buddy can also encourage you to keep going. It's also a great way to bond with a friend or family member.

If you're ever unsure about starting a new exercise routine or you suffer from health conditions, speak to your doctor first. They will recommend exercises you can do according to your health.

Personal Hygiene

Personal hygiene is more than just looking clean—it's essential for your overall health and well-being. Starting your day with a refreshing shower cleans your body, invigorates your mind, and sets a positive tone for your day ahead. Brushing your teeth is not only about a bright smile; it's a crucial step in preventing dental issues and keeping your teeth healthy. Adding regular flossing to your dental routine helps keep those hard-to-reach places clean, reducing the risk of getting cavities or gum disease.

Handwashing is a simple but effective way to stop germs from spreading. Before having a meal and after using the bathroom, taking a moment to wash your hands can significantly reduce your risk of getting infections and illnesses.

Skincare Routines

Skincare isn't just for girls. It's important to look after your skin because a daily routine can keep it healthy and spare you pain when it comes to developing rashes and other skin irritations. Here are some simple steps to keep your skin healthy:

1. Begin by cleansing your face with a gentle cleanser suitable for your skin type. This removes impurities and excess oil.
2. Follow cleansing with a toner to balance your skin's pH levels and tighten pores.
3. Apply a moisturizer to keep your skin hydrated, preventing dryness and promoting a soft, supple complexion.
4. Don't forget to use sunscreen with at least SPF 30 during the day to shield your skin from harmful UV rays and reduce the risk of sun damage.

Embarking on a skincare journey isn't only about looking good; it's also about keeping your skin healthy as you get older. If you pay more attention to your skin, you'll notice sooner if something serious is wrong, for example, potential skin cancer.

Haircare

Maybe you don't pay that much attention to your hair or don't have that much of it, but the truth is your hair needs your love and attention, too. Beautiful, attractive hair is, after all, a confidence booster.

A haircare routine helps keep your locks clean, healthy, and manageable. Use a shampoo and conditioner designed for your hair type. If you have oily hair, use a clarifying shampoo; for dry hair, choose a hydrating conditioner. You need to wash your hair regularly, but don't overdo it, as it can strip its natural oils, and you'll end up with dry hair.

Oral Health and Dental Care

It's vital to take care of your teeth from a young age. After all, you only get one set of teeth that will last you a lifetime, and you don't want to undergo painful and expensive dental procedures if you don't have to.

Brush your teeth at least twice a day with fluoride toothpaste and a soft-bristle toothbrush. Adopt proper brushing techniques by gently angling the brush toward your gum line and then cleaning each tooth thoroughly with circular motions. An electric toothbrush is usually more effective for plaque removal. However, doing it the old-fashioned manual way is fine, too.

Flossing is equally important; it reaches areas between your teeth that you could miss while brushing. It should be part of your daily routine to prevent plaque buildup and reduce the risk of gum disease.

Visit your dentist at least twice a year for cleanings and examinations. If you experience toothaches or sensitivity, you should contact your dentist for an appointment.

Your Personal Style

When it comes to clothes, you should start by wearing items that fit you properly. You should also wear the right clothes for the right occasion. For example, formal wear such as tuxedos and evening gowns are appropriate for events such as weddings or upscale dinners.

Maybe you don't have that many formal events you have to attend at the moment, but it's good to know how to dress.

If you have the right basics in your closet, you can create a look for every occasion. Dress shirts in different colors can be paired with colored pants, like navy or khaki, to create casual and semi-formal looks.

Suit jackets are useful items that can give your jeans and T-shirt a snazzier look.

Let's not forget about footwear. A classic pair of black or brown dress shoes can be used for formal work events, but they're also date night material and can help you make a killer impression on the girl of your dreams.

You don't need a closet that's bursting at the seams. You just need the right mix of stylish and simple clothes, and you'll be ready for anything.

Stress Management

Chronic stress is bad for your physical and mental health. Before you can manage your stress levels, you need to recognize the signs that you're stressed.

The Signs

You'll probably first experience physical signs when you become stressed, so you should pay attention to your body. You could develop a headache or stomach ache, your muscles could be tense and stiff, and you could be tired all the time. These are all ways your body reacts to stress.

Stress also leads to emotional changes. You could feel more irritable, angry, sad, and even anxious. Instead of taking your negative feelings out on others, you should acknowledge them and explore what could be causing them.

Your behavior could also change; for example, you could withdraw from activities you used to enjoy. You may also struggle to concentrate and experience changes in your eating or sleeping habits. These are all signs that stress is affecting you.

Dealing With Stress

It's normal to feel stressed from time to time, but you should be able to recognize when it's becoming overwhelming and then take steps to address it. You can effectively manage stress through effective coping mechanisms.

So, how do you deal with it now that you've determined you're stressed? There are quite a few things you can do, and you'll have to figure out what works best for you:

- When it comes to dealing with stress, getting enough sleep is probably one of the most important things you can do. Going without sleep will make you grumpy and affect your concentration. Try to get at least eight hours every night.
- Getting enough exercise will also get you through rough times. Make sure you get around 60 minutes most days.
- Good communication skills will also help you deal with stress. If you have a problem with someone, talk to them about it. If you have a problem you can't solve yourself, talk to a trusted adult, like one of your parents, about it.
- It's fun to hang out with your friends and parties, but make sure you also have some unstructured leisure

time to relax and do whatever you feel like. You need time for yourself.

- Spending time outside can reduce your stress levels, so go on a camping trip with your friends or family members. Don't stress if you can't do something as extensive as that; time spent in the garden at home or even in the park will already help you feel better.
- Writing can reduce mental stress, and writing in a journal can help you express your emotions constructively. If you're not really a writer, you can also draw pictures. If you don't enjoy writing in books but technology is your thing, why not keep an electronic journal on one of your digital devices? Who knows, one day, you might even be able to compile your thoughts into the next bestseller.
- This may not sound like fun, but limit your screen time and do a digital detox from time to time. Too much time online can also lead to stress.

Coping With Your Emotions

Emotional intelligence might not sound that exciting, but mastering these skills can help you get ahead in life.

What exactly does it mean to cope with emotions? It's all about understanding, managing, and expressing your feelings healthily. That means recognizing what you're feeling, figuring out why you're feeling that way, and finding constructive ways to deal with those emotions. You also need to be able to name your emotions, which will help you recognize what you are feeling; for example, sad, angry, or scared.

You could be feeling stressed about a big test coming up. Instead of freaking out and letting that stress overwhelm you, take a step back, acknowledge how you're feeling, and then come up with a plan to tackle studying in a calm and focused way. That's a good example of how to cope with your emotions.

Emotional intelligence takes things to the next level. It's not just about managing your own emotions; it's also about understanding and navigating the emotions of others. That means putting yourself in someone else's shoes, recognizing what they're feeling, and responding in a way that shows you understand and care.

Think about it: If your buddy is going through a tough time, being emotionally intelligent means being there for them, listening to what they have to say, and offering support and empathy. It's about being a good friend and building stronger connections with the people around you.

Developing these skills isn't a one-time thing. It's an ongoing process that takes practice and commitment. It will help you navigate life's ups and downs with more grace and resilience, improve your relationships, and make you a better friend, son, and overall fantastic human being.

So, don't underestimate the power of emotional intelligence and coping with emotions. Embrace these skills and practice them every day.

Mental Health

Understanding your mental health is crucial, and it's totally okay not to feel okay sometimes. We all have those moments when things feel off, and we don't know how to feel better. That's fine. However, it's important to know that you're not alone and there are people you can turn to for support, whether it's family, friends, teachers, or even a counselor. If your feelings get really bad, don't keep them to yourself; make sure you talk about them to someone.

Let's talk about the difficult feelings you think you can handle yourself. One way to tackle these feelings is by simply acknowledging them. Take a moment to check in with yourself and identify what you're feeling. Are you feeling sad, anxious, or overwhelmed? Once you've identified your feelings and can name them, try to understand why you might be feeling that way. Maybe something happened that triggered those emotions, or maybe it's just a rough day. If you're still struggling to identify your feelings or to determine why you feel this way, write them down.

Now, here's the important part: How do you get rid of that funky feeling? One thing you can try is doing something that usually brings you joy or relaxation. It could be listening to your favorite music, going for a walk, playing a sport, or even talking to a friend. Sometimes, just getting out of your head and focusing on something else can help lift your mood.

And remember, you're not alone in this. There are plenty of people who care about you and want to help. Don't hesitate to reach out to someone you trust if your feelings are getting overwhelming. Whether it's confiding in a friend, family member, or a professional, talking about what you're going through can make a world of difference.

Screen Time

We all love using our devices, whether gaming, scrolling through social media, or binge-watching our favorite shows. And hey, there's nothing wrong with that! However, it's essential to use screen time effectively, especially during the holiday season when we might find ourselves glued to our screens for longer periods.

First things first, it's crucial to recognize when it's appropriate to have longer screen times and when it's time to minimize it. Sure, holidays are a great time to relax and catch up on our favorite games or shows, but we also need to balance it out with other activities. So, before diving into hours of screen time, ask yourself if there are other things you could be doing to make the most of your holiday break, such as hiking with your friends or taking your dog to the park.

Now, let's talk about minimizing screen time when needed. Sometimes, we get so caught up in our digital worlds that we forget to take breaks and engage in real-life activities. That's why it's essential to set boundaries and schedule time away from screens. Whether going for a walk, hanging out with friends, or pursuing a hobby, find activities that allow you to take a break from screens and recharge.

Screen time can be entertaining, but it's all about finding the right balance. So, during the holiday season, enjoy your time online, but also take breaks and engage in other activities.

Digital Detox

Sometimes, we need to give ourselves a longer break from technology and give ourselves a digital detox.

Why is this so important? First, spending too much time staring at screens can mess with our sleep patterns. You know how sometimes you're up way past your bedtime scrolling through TikTok or playing games? All that screen time can make it much more difficult to fall asleep, which means you won't function at your best the next day.

Too much screen time can also affect your mental health. Spending hours on social media comparing yourself to others or getting sucked into drama can mess with your mind. Sometimes, you have to focus on real-life interactions instead of living in the digital world all the time.

Plus, too much screen time can make us feel isolated. It may sound strange because we're always connected online, but spending too much time on screens can make us feel lonely and disconnected from the real world. It's important to take breaks and spend time with friends and family in person.

How do you do a digital detox? It's simple. Take a break from your devices for a few hours or even a whole day if you can. Several days away is even better; for example, if you go camping where there is no reception. Just let your friends know beforehand that you won't be able to answer their messages. Go outside, hang out with friends, or start a new hobby. You'll feel much better after a good stretch of time away from your screen.

Key Takeaways

- Enough sleep, balanced nutrition, and regular exercise are essential for overall health and development.
- Consistent sleep patterns and a bedtime routine are crucial for quality sleep.
- Tips for getting better sleep include avoiding screens before bed, creating a comfortable sleeping environment, and managing caffeine intake.

- A balanced diet with fruits, vegetables, lean proteins, whole grains, and healthy fats will boost your growth and energy levels.
- Aim for at least 30 minutes to an hour of exercise most days, engaging in activities you enjoy.
- Recognizing signs of stress is crucial for managing it effectively.
- Acknowledging and understanding emotions is vital for your mental well-being.
- Balancing screen time with real-life activities is essential for well-rounded development.
- Taking regular breaks from technology, or digital detox, is beneficial for sleep, mental health, and social connection.

In Chapter 7, we'll discuss healthy relationships and how to form them.

CHAPTER 7:

RELATIONSHIPS

Imagine your relationship as a cozy space where you can share anything without judgment. It's all about talking openly and really listening to each other. Trust is the glue that holds everything together, so be someone your friends can rely on. Share your thoughts and celebrate each other's uniqueness to build trust.

Spending quality time together will make your connection stronger. Celebrate the happy times and have empathy for each other when times get tough. Be an active listener and show your friends that they are important to you.

Understanding each other's feelings and working through conflicts together will make your relationship a safe and supportive place. That's the recipe for a relationship that survives, thrives, and creates strong, lasting bonds.

Relationship ABCs

Our relationships with others are at the core of our life experiences. Our connections with our friends, family members, teachers, and romantic partners shape our lives in meaningful ways.

Relationships provide support, companionship, and a sense of belonging, which are essential for your personal growth and emotional well-being. People with strong social networks are usually happier, more resilient, and better able to deal with challenges.

Types of Relationships

Throughout our lives, we'll have relationships with different kinds of people that will add different layers of meaning to our lives. Let's take a look at the types of relationships we all experience:

Family

The first relationships in your life will be with your family members—your parents, siblings, grandparents, and other relatives. You will learn the foundations of healthy behavior from your family. Family relationships should be characterized by unconditional love, support, and shared experiences. They can provide a sense of belonging and security, but they can come with many challenges, such as disagreements and frustrations. A healthy family will allow you to explore the dynamics of authority, independence, and autonomy in your family relationships.

Friends

As a teenager, friendships are an important part of your life. They offer companionship, camaraderie, and a support system outside the family unit. However, you also have to be careful not to make bad friends who want to take you down the wrong road; you should always stand up for yourself and never do things you don't want to do. Peer pressure has played a negative role in many teenagers' lives.

Friendships among teenage boys often revolve around shared interests, activities, and experiences. These relationships provide opportunities for socialization, emotional support, and personal growth. Learning to deal with your relationships as a teenager can help you develop social skills and emotional resilience.

Teachers

A good relationship with your teachers is important in your academic and personal development.

Teachers can be your mentors, guides, and role models, offering support, encouragement, and guidance. These relationships are characterized by mutual respect, trust, and communication. However, you could also experience miscommunication and conflicts with your teachers.

Romantic Partners

Romantic relationships introduce you to the complexities of love, intimacy, and commitment. These connections involve emotional, intellectual, and often physical bonds with a romantic partner.

Romantic relationships can also be challenging, and you can experience feelings of infatuation, attraction, and jealousy.

Healthy romantic relationships are built on mutual respect, trust, communication, and consent. You'll learn about boundaries, empathy, and emotional regulation through your romantic experiences.

There Are Two Sides to Relationships

It's also important to remember that all relationships are two-sided. It involves both you and another person and is a matter of give and take.

You both contribute to the relationship in different ways. For example, in a friendship, you and your friend share your thoughts, feelings, and experiences. You support each other during tough times and celebrate together during good times. It's about what you get from the relationship and what you give.

When you're in a relationship, you have a responsibility to the other person. Your actions and words affect them, just like theirs affect you. It's important to be mindful of how you treat the other person and to take responsibility for your behavior. Whether it's being honest, respectful, or supportive, your actions shape the relationship.

Good communication is key to any relationship. It's about expressing yourself and listening to the other person. You need to understand their perspective, feelings, and needs. By communicating openly and honestly, you can strengthen your relationships and resolve conflicts more effectively.

Respect goes both ways in a relationship. You should respect the other person's boundaries, opinions, and feelings, just as you expect them to respect yours. Treating each other with kindness and consideration creates a healthy and positive connection.

Think of your relationship as a team effort. You and the other person are on the same team, working together toward common goals. Whether supporting each other's dreams, solving problems, or simply enjoying each other's company, you're in it together.

Showing Respect

Respect is the cornerstone of healthy relationships, especially if you want to keep them long-term.

Respect is about showing you care and understanding where someone else is coming from. The golden rule is to treat others the way you want to be treated. Respect helps you make friends, get along with family, and even deal with teachers and other grown-ups. If you treat others well and like you want to be treated, you'll gain their respect.

How to Show Respect

How do you show respect to others? It might seem like a bit of an abstract idea. You can show respect by acting in the following ways:

- When someone's talking, really tune in and show them you're paying attention. Don't interrupt them, but also don't zone out. Everyone knows you're not really listening when you get that blank look on your face.
- We're all different, so it's cool to hear diverse opinions and see things from other angles. Do your best to keep an open mind.
- Be honest, but do it respectfully—no need for harsh words or being sneaky. Think carefully before you respond to others.
- Put yourself in the shoes of others and think about how they're feeling or what they need.
- Treat others' belongings like you'd want yours treated. It's not okay to mess with someone else's stuff without permission.

Dealing With Disrespect

How do you react when someone is really awful to you and treats you with total disrespect?

- Sometimes, it's easiest just to brush them off. Ignore them and don't give attention to their disrespectful ways.
- If it's getting to be too much, don't be afraid to leave the situation. You've got better things to do than deal with negativity.
- If you need to, don't hold back from telling them how you feel and setting some boundaries.
- If things get too hectic, reach out to an adult for support.

Building Trust

If you are real, honest, and reliable in your relationships, they'll become stronger with time.

Imagine having someone in your corner who's got your back no matter what. You know that the other person has your best interests at heart. Trusting someone is like saying, "I believe in you, and I know you won't let me down."

When Trust Takes a Hit

When someone breaks your trust, it can feel like a punch in the gut. You could start questioning the entire relationship.

Broken trust hurts, plain and simple. Your relationship has been damaged, and you'll have to figure out if it's fixable.

Rebuilding Trust

Once trust has been broken, it can take a lot of hard work to rebuild. It might not be as simple as saying sorry and then wanting to move on. Everyone involved in breaking the trust should own up to their mistakes, be honest about what happened, and then show commitment to improving things. Trust can be restored if everyone involved is willing to work at it.

SETTING BOUNDARIES

Setting boundaries is an important part of healthy relationships. As a teenager, you're still discovering your identity and understanding your rights and limits. Boundaries are the invisible lines that define what is acceptable and respectful in various aspects of your life. We'll look at the significance of boundaries, when to set them, and how to assert them confidently.

How to Understand Boundaries

Boundaries are like the fences around your yard; they define your personal space, emotions, and values.

They can be physical, emotional, or even digital. Physical boundaries involve your personal space and touch. Emotional boundaries are about your feelings, thoughts, and beliefs. Digital boundaries revolve around your online presence and interactions. Setting digital boundaries is still a relatively new thing, but it's becoming increasingly important in our digital world.

Setting and respecting boundaries is not about building walls but fostering mutual respect and understanding. Boundaries help you feel safe, valued, and in control of your own life. You're showing respect for yourself by setting boundaries and not allowing others to take advantage of you.

When to Set Boundaries

When it comes to knowing when to set boundaries, you have to trust your instincts. If someone in your life is making you feel uncomfortable and crossing the line, it's time to set boundaries. It's always okay to say no and assert your needs.

Speak Up

When someone has crossed your boundaries, you need to speak up. You might feel hesitant because you're afraid of confrontation, but expressing discomfort is vital for your well-being. Be assertive, clear, and respectful when communicating your boundaries. Use "I" statements to express your feelings and needs. For example, "I feel uncomfortable when you joke about my appearance. Please stop."

Seek Support

If you're struggling to assert your boundaries, get support from friends, adults in your life, or a counselor. They can guide you and offer support.

Romantic Relationships

Building and keeping strong relationships is a bit like tending to a garden. You've got to plant the seeds, water them, and give them sunlight. That initial spark you feel when you connect with someone is like planting those seeds—it's exciting and full of possibilities. But, just like plants need care, relationships need attention and effort to grow.

Imagine you and your friend or partner as a team. You work together to navigate through the ups and downs, like teammates in a game. Open communication helps you understand each other better. Like any team, there will be challenges, but overcoming them together strengthens the bond. It's the little things, like remembering their favorite snack or being there during tough times, that create a lasting connection. A mix of care, communication, and shared experiences is the best strategy for forming strong and lasting connections.

Dating and romance are almost like an ever-changing story. When you connect with someone at first, you're full of curiosity and excitement about what might happen. Dating with intention is about being clear on your values, expectations, and the kind of relationship you're looking for. You're not only playing around but looking for a lasting connection.

Integrity in dating involves being truthful about who you are and what you're seeking. Being honest about your feelings and intentions and being open about your past adds depth to the story you're creating together. If you mislead someone about what you're looking for, the relationship won't last long. It's about building a connection on a foundation of trust and mutual understanding.

Individual Pace

When it comes to romantic relationships, it's also important to understand that everyone moves at their own pace. Society always has ideas about what you should be doing and when, but you need to honor your own feelings and boundaries. You might feel that you're not ready for a romantic relationship as a teenager, and that's fine. If you want to focus on your studies and have fun with your friends, you can leave romantic relationships for when you're older.

The Dos and Don'ts of Romantic Relationships

When you're in a romantic relationship for the first time, you might not always be sure how to react and how to treat your partner to get the most out of your relationship.

Here are some tips to keep you on the right track:

- Honest communication is the cornerstone of any healthy relationship. Share your thoughts, feelings, and concerns with your partner and encourage them to do the same. Don't deal with negative feelings in a passive-aggressive way.
- Pay attention to any behaviors or patterns that make you feel uncomfortable or disrespected. Trust your instincts and deal with issues early on. It's also useful to know the signs of a toxic relationship.
- You need to know your boundaries in a relationship and understand and respect your partner's boundaries. For example, how far are you and your partner willing to go when it comes to intimacy? Boundaries will help both of you feel safe, secure, and respected.
- While it's natural to compromise and make sacrifices in a relationship, it's important to maintain your sense of self and pursue your passions and interests. One person should also not be giving up everything in the relationship. You need to maintain your

individuality and not just become the other half of something.

- Treat your partner with the same level of respect and kindness you expect in return. Value their opinions, feelings, and autonomy. Treat your partner with kindness, understanding, and appreciation.
- Physical intimacy should occur only when both partners are ready and comfortable. Take the time to build trust and emotional connection before you get to the physical, no matter how tempting it might seem.
- Seek to understand your partner's perspective, experiences, and emotions. Empathy fosters deeper connections and strengthens the bond between partners.

Signs of Toxicity and Abuse in Romantic Relationships

Unfortunately, there's always the likelihood that we might end up in a toxic relationship with someone.

The following signs are what we call "red flags" and will tell you when something is wrong in a relationship:

- An abusive partner usually has controlling tendencies, such as isolating the victim from friends and family or monitoring their communications without consent; for example, your partner could try to read your messages on your phone or your emails because they don't trust you.

- The abusive partner might make you feel as if you're to blame for the bad treatment they're giving you. They don't take responsibility for their actions.
- You know your relationship has become abusive when your partner calls you names, threatens you, or mistreats you emotionally in other ways.
- Hitting, slapping, pushing, or damaging property are also abusive actions.
- The abusive partner may try to control your money by taking it from you or expecting you to spend it all on them.
- Invading personal space or using aggressive body language creates an atmosphere of fear.
- The abuser could have mood swings that they take out on you. Rapid shifts between kindness and aggression, along with explosive anger reactions, indicate an unstable relationship.
- Abusers often downplay the severity of their actions, engage in denial or blame-shifting, and minimize the impact of their behavior.

If you or someone you know is experiencing abuse, seeking help from friends, family, or professionals is essential.

KEY TAKEAWAYS

- Relationships are vital in life, offering support, companionship, and a sense of belonging.
- Healthy family relationships are built on unconditional love, support, and shared experiences, while friendships offer companionship, camaraderie, and support outside the family unit.
- Romantic relationships introduce the complexities of love, intimacy, and commitment, requiring mutual respect, trust, communication, and consent.
- All relationships are two-sided, involve give and take, and require good communication, respect, and empathy.
- Respect is crucial in maintaining healthy relationships.
- Trust forms the foundation of strong relationships, built through honesty, reliability, and belief in the other person.
- Setting boundaries is important for protecting your personal space and emotions.
- Signs of toxicity and abuse in romantic relationships include controlling behavior, blaming the victim, verbal or physical abuse, financial control, invasion of personal space, mood swings, and denial or minimization of abusive behavior.

In Chapter 8, we'll look at moving into adulthood and the new responsibilities you'll get along the way.

CHAPTER 8:

INDEPENDENCE AND RESPONSIBILITIES

Your teenage years are a thrilling journey of self-discovery and growth. One of the key aspects of this journey is understanding the significance of accountability, gaining independence, and embracing lifelong learning.

Taking responsibility for your actions is crucial in shaping your character and building trust with others. Let's discuss how you can gradually gain independence, make your own decisions, and carve your path in the world while respecting the guidance of those who care about you.

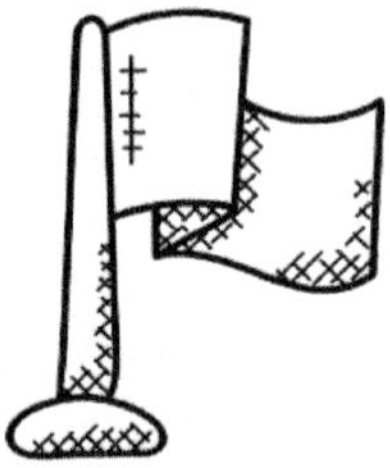

INTRODUCTION TO INDEPENDENCE

What does it mean to be independent? If you're independent, you can care for yourself and make your own decisions without relying on others for everything. It's about being self-sufficient and responsible for your actions.

Developing independence is a rite of passage and a crucial step toward adulthood.

So, how can you start your journey to becoming responsible and self-sufficient?

At home, independence might mean taking on tasks such as cooking, cleaning, or doing your laundry. These may seem like small chores, but they're essential for learning to take care of yourself and contribute to your household. By mastering these skills, you're not only lightening the load for your family but also gaining valuable life skills that will serve you well in the future. Trust me, you'll be glad you know how to do all these things once you're on your own, out there in the world.

When it comes to school, your independence can take on a slightly different form. It's about managing your time effectively, completing assignments on time, and studying for exams independently. This means taking ownership of your education and prioritizing your responsibilities as a student. By staying organized and disciplined, you'll excel academically and develop the resilience and self-discipline you need to succeed in just about anything.

Remember, independence doesn't mean you have to do everything on your own. It's okay to ask for help when you need it and ask adults for guidance. However, it's important to strike a balance between relying on others and taking the initiative to tackle challenges on your own.

Managing Time for Independence

Time management is the secret ingredient that helps you balance your responsibilities effectively, ensuring you have enough time for everything that matters in your life.

Why is time management so crucial? Imagine this: You have homework to complete, chores at home, and maybe even extracurricular activities or hobbies you enjoy. Without proper time management, it's easy to feel overwhelmed, and you could struggle to juggle everything on your plate. But fear not because mastering the art of time management will not only help you stay on top of your tasks but also give you the freedom to pursue your passions and goals.

One of the key aspects of time management is prioritization. It's important to identify which tasks are most urgent and tackle them first. For example, if you have a big assignment due tomorrow, it makes sense to prioritize studying for that rather than watching a TV series or playing online games. By prioritizing your tasks, you ensure you're making the most of your time and focusing on what truly matters.

Another strategy for effective time management is creating a schedule or a to-do list. This allows you to visualize your day and allocate time for each task accordingly. Whether you prefer using a planner, a smartphone app, or a simple pen and paper, find a method that works for you and stick to it. Having a schedule helps you stay organized and will hold you accountable for how you spend your time.

It's vital to recognize that balance is key. There will be times when you'll need to pay more attention to certain responsibilities than others. For example, during exam week, you may need to devote more time to studying and less time to leisure activities. Learning to adapt and prioritize your time based on the demands of each situation is a skill you'll also be able to use for the rest of your life.

Time Management Tools

Time management tools can help you stay on top of your game and make the most of your time.

Think of time management tools like your personal assistants—they're there to help you stay organized and get stuff done. Whether it's apps on your phone or a good old-fashioned planner, these tools come in all shapes and sizes, and you can choose whatever option works for you.

Why are they so awesome? They're designed to help you plan your tasks, set goals, and organize your schedule. Whether you need to tackle school assignments, plan out your workouts, or simply keep track of your social plans, these tools have your back.

And here's the best part: They're all about helping you be more productive and efficient. Whether you're using an app or software or just jotting things down on paper, these tools give you a structure to manage your to-dos, plan your time, and work toward your goals.

The goal here is to help you use your time wisely, avoid procrastination, and get stuff done—both in your personal life and at school or work.

So, whether you're a digital whiz who loves using apps or more of a pen-and-paper kind of guy, there's a time management tool out there that's perfect for you. Try them all until you find the one that works for you.

TAKING RESPONSIBILITY

Taking responsibility as you move through your teenage years becomes increasingly important. Unlike when you were younger, you won't always have your parents to fall back on. It's time to step up and own your actions like a responsible person.

The benefit of showing yourself to be a responsible person is that your parents will also trust you to do more things on your own.

What does taking responsibility really mean? It's about being accountable for your choices and actions and their consequences. You have to be able to acknowledge when you've made a mistake or fallen short, and you need to take steps to make things right. This isn't always easy, but it's a crucial part of growing up and becoming a mature adult.

Accountability isn't just about admitting when you're wrong; it's also about learning from your experiences. We all make mistakes—it's part of being human. But what sets you apart is how you respond to those mistakes. By reflecting on what went wrong and how you can do better next time, you show maturity and growth.

Let's break it down with a simple example: doing your own laundry. Sure, it might seem like a small thing, but it's a big step toward independence and responsibility. By taking charge of your laundry, you're ensuring that you always have clean clothes for school and other activities. Plus, you're showing your parents that you're capable of handling tasks on your own and contributing to the household.

But responsibility isn't just about chores—it's about how you conduct yourself in all aspects of your life. Whether it's being punctual for appointments, honoring commitments, or treating others with respect, every action you take shapes your character and builds your reputation.

So, embrace the responsibility with open arms. Learn from your mistakes, take ownership of your actions, and strive to be the best version of yourself. Ultimately, these qualities will set you up for success in all areas of your life.

Building Routines

Let's talk about routines and why they're super important for you. You might think routines are just for adults, but trust me, they can benefit everyone, including you.

First off, let's talk about why routines matter. Maybe your day is like a well-oiled machine. You wake up, brush your teeth, grab breakfast, head to school, tackle homework, maybe hit the gym, then wind down for bed. Having a routine like this might sound boring at first, but it's actually pretty awesome!

Routine gives you stability. It's like having a road map for your day. When you know what to expect, it can help you feel more in control and less stressed. Plus, it frees up mental space because you don't have to constantly figure out what to do next.

Having a routine doesn't mean you're stuck in a rigid schedule. Instead, you can take charge of your day and make your routines work for you. When you follow a routine, you're showing you can manage your time and take care of yourself without relying on others to tell you what to do.

You could have a routine where you set aside time every day to work on your hobbies or passions. Maybe you're into gaming, playing sports, or practicing music. Building this into your routine allows you to pursue your interests and develop your skills independently.

How do you build a routine? Start by identifying what's important and what you want to achieve. Then, map out your day accordingly, making sure to include time for school, hobbies, socializing, and self-care. Be flexible and open to adjustments as needed, but stick to the basics to maintain that sense of stability.

In a nutshell, routines are your secret weapon for a successful and fulfilling teenage life. They give you stability and independence and help you achieve your goals—all while keeping things positive and empowering. Having goals will change your life for the better.

Solving Problems

Being able to solve problems is also an important part of becoming responsible and more independent.

Problem-solving is like being a detective in your own life: You encounter a mystery, and it's up to you to figure out the best way to solve it. First, you have to identify the problem. Clearly understand what's not working or what challenge you're facing.

Once you've got a handle on the problem, break it down. Think of it like breaking a big task into smaller, more manageable steps. It makes the whole process less overwhelming. Look at each piece of the puzzle separately to find out where things might be going wrong.

Be creative with solutions and think outside the box. You might have to approach the problem from different angles.

Don't be afraid to ask others for advice. Other people could help you gain a fresh perspective. Sometimes, a collaborative effort can unveil solutions you might not have thought about on your own.

Try different solutions until you find something that works. Use the knowledge you gained from each attempt to refine your strategy. Resilience is key, so keep trying and moving forward.

Making Decisions

Decision-making means you have to navigate through the choices life throws at you. It's about making up your mind when you're faced with certain options. If you can make sensible decisions fast, it will also help your problem-solving abilities.

Let's break decision-making down in simpler terms:

- You first need to understand what decision you need to make and what you want to achieve with it.

- Consider the available options. Picture it as looking at a menu—each dish represents a different choice. What are the potential benefits, and what are the risks or downsides of every option?
- Listen to your gut feeling. Sometimes, that little voice inside your head or that feeling in your stomach can guide you. If something feels right or wrong, it's worth paying attention to.
- Break down the decision into smaller parts if needed. Tackling it step by step can make it more manageable.
- Once you've made a decision, commit to it. It's like choosing a path on a map—once you've decided, start walking that way. Trust your judgment and give it your best shot.

Not every decision has to be perfect. Life is a journey of learning, especially when you move from childhood into adulthood. Making decisions is just part of that adventure. If things don't turn out as planned, view it as an opportunity to grow and adapt.

Making Mistakes

Mistakes are a natural part of life, like taking a few wrong turns before finding the right path. Every time you make a decision, it's also possible that you'll make a wrong one, and it will end up being a mistake.

Think of your mistakes as stepping stones on your way to success. Often, we can only see what went wrong in a certain situation when we've gained some distance from it and look back.

Everyone makes mistakes. It's how your brain learns, and it could even lead to discoveries. If you work to improve something you did wrong, it could end up being a great invention that no one else ever thought of. Just imagine that!

Don't be too hard on yourself when you make an error. You should aim to learn from your errors and become better in the process. If you experience setbacks, ask yourself what you can learn from them and how you can do things differently next time.

Remember, the key is resilience. When faced with a mistake, don't give up; see it as a growth opportunity that will eventually lead to success. A mistake is just a temporary detour from success.

Techniques for Developing Emotional Strength and Resilience

Resilience is all about being tough, bouncing back from difficult stuff, and not letting life's challenges knock you down. You're almost like a hero in the movies who can handle things life throws at you.

Let's be clear: You're going to face setbacks, whether it's a bad grade, a breakup, or just feeling down in the dumps.

However, if you're resilient, those setbacks won't hold you back.

Instead, it's about dusting yourself off, picking yourself up, and pushing forward—even when things get tough. It's about believing in yourself and staying positive.

And here's the cool part: Resilience isn't something you're born with—it's something you can develop and strengthen over time. It's like a muscle—the more you work it out, the stronger it gets.

How do you build resilience? It's all about having a positive attitude, staying connected with friends and family, and learning from your experiences. It's also about taking care of yourself—physically, mentally, and emotionally—and asking for help when you need it.

It's okay to struggle sometimes. We're all human, and nobody's perfect.

Building emotional strength and resilience is a gradual process, and you can start learning these skills from early childhood. Don't worry too much if your resilience is not quite up to scratch yet; you can improve it throughout your life.

The following techniques will boost your emotional well-being and resilience:

- Make mindfulness practices part of your daily routine, such as meditation or deep-breathing exercises. Focus on the present moment, experiencing your thoughts and feelings without judging yourself.

- Challenge negative thoughts and replace them with positive affirmations. For example, instead of believing you'll never be able to do something, tell yourself you'll learn how to do it.
- Share your thoughts and feelings with your family and friends. Be open to receiving support from others. If you feel depressed or anxious, or you're experiencing peer pressure, you shouldn't be trying to manage these issues on your own.
- Celebrate your small victories to boost your confidence and motivation. For example, if you have achieved part of your main goal, do something to celebrate, even if you just reward yourself with your favorite snack.
- Change is a natural part of life. Develop flexible thinking and adapt the way you deal with challenges. For example, if you haven't prepared enough for a test, spend more time studying for your next test.
- Treat yourself with kindness and understanding, especially during difficult times. If you push yourself too hard, especially when you're ill, it could just cause you to burn out.

- Prioritize regular exercise, adequate sleep, and a balanced diet. Your physical well-being contributes to emotional resilience.
- View challenges as opportunities for personal growth. Reflect on past difficulties and acknowledge the lessons learned from them. Have you made mistakes in the past that have taught you something valuable?
- Break down problems into manageable parts. Identify potential solutions and take practical steps to address challenges.
- Pursue activities that bring you joy and fulfillment. Engaging in hobbies provides an outlet for stress and enhances emotional well-being.
- Set clear boundaries to protect your emotional energy. Learn to say no when necessary and prioritize self-care. Your mental health will be better if you can stand up for yourself.

Transitioning to Adulthood

As you gear up for adulthood, the skills you've learned in this guide will give you a head start.

The routines you've built, the emotions you've learned to manage, and the challenges you've faced have all taught you valuable lessons that will come in handy as you transition into adulthood.

Routines may seem boring at first, but they're the secret to a successful life. Whether it's getting into the habit of doing your homework at a certain time, exercising every day, or even just having a solid morning routine, sticking to these habits will set you up for success.

There is also the whole emotional intelligence thing. Understanding your own emotions and managing them, as well as the ability to understand the emotions of those around you, can help you a great deal when it comes to forming healthy relationships. It'll help you navigate tough situations, communicate better with others, and stay cool under pressure—whether you're dealing with a tricky boss, a challenging relationship, or the stresses of adulting.

Let's not forget about problem-solving. Life often throws unexpected surprises at us, not all of them good, and being able to think on your feet and come up with creative solutions is key. Whether it's fixing a flat tire, figuring out which career you want to follow, or tackling a tough math problem, those problem-solving skills will be useful.

Adulthood isn't just about having a bunch of skills in your back pocket. It's also about staying hungry for learning and growth and constantly pushing yourself to be better. Whether it's pursuing further education, learning a new skill, or stepping out of your comfort zone, you should always challenge yourself to grow and evolve.

Building strong relationships with friends, mentors, and peers will be crucial as you navigate the ups and downs of adulthood. So, stay connected, lean on your support network when you need to, and never underestimate the power of having good people in your corner.

Key Takeaways

- Independence means you're self-sufficient and responsible for your actions.
- Time management is essential for balancing responsibilities, prioritizing tasks, and pursuing passions.
- Time management tools such as apps or planners assist in organizing tasks and schedules efficiently.
- Taking responsibility means owning actions, learning from mistakes, and contributing positively to various aspects of life.
- Routine building provides stability, independence, and goal achievement.

- Problem-solving and decision-making skills are essential for navigating challenges and making informed choices.
- Making mistakes is part of learning and growth; resilience helps you bounce back from setbacks.
- Transitioning to adulthood involves utilizing learned skills such as routines, emotional intelligence, problem-solving, and maintaining strong relationships for personal and professional success.

Well, you've got to the end of the book. Thank you so much for reading! I have thoroughly enjoyed writing this book, and truly hope you've enjoyed it, have found value in it and most importantly, learnt skills that you'll use for the rest of your life. If you have, it would be very greatly appreciated if you could head over to Amazon to leave a review! Leaving a review is the best way to support this book and ensure we can make more books to help others just like you.

Your feedback lets me know how I've done and what I can improve on within my next book! Oh talking about my next book, remember that QR code at the start which gives you access to all of the worksheets specific to this book? Well, I'll also let you know when the next book is out and when it is available at a discount! Anyway, back to the review...

Simply scan this QR code with your phone, and you will be taken to the book's review page.

Alternatively, to leave a review without scanning this QR code:

- Head over to this book's page on Amazon or find it through your purchases
- Scroll down towards the bottom of the page and click on the button that says "Write a Customer Review"
- You can simply leave a star rating out of 5, or write a short review!

Thanks everyone! Your support is greatly appreciated!

CONCLUSION

Congratulations on reaching the end of this book. Throughout this empowering journey, you've built the life skills to handle your teenage years effectively and successfully complete your journey into adulthood.

You've gone through some serious training in this book that will help you become the best version of yourself during your journey through puberty. You've become more confident in dealing with all kinds of challenges, including peer pressure, and you're now prepared to deal with various challenges that might come your way.

You have the mental strength to take control of your own personal development, and you know you have to keep reaching for your dreams. Remember, your potential is limitless, and you can make your mark in the world.

KEY TAKEAWAYS

This book taught you the following:

- You've delved into the depths of your identity, embracing the changes to your body and mind during puberty while embarking on a journey of self-exploration.

- Armed with techniques to boost your self-esteem, you've learned to navigate peer pressure with resilience and stand tall when facing challenges.
- By cultivating awareness and presence, you've honed the ability to stay grounded and centered amidst life's twists and turns, fostering mental clarity and well-being.
- You've mastered the art of setting goals, prioritizing tasks, and adapting to change with grace and efficiency, which will maximize your potential for success.
- With a solid foundation in financial literacy, including budgeting, saving, and managing debt, you're well-prepared to take charge of your financial future. Information about side hustles has shown you that there are all kinds of possibilities and that you can even create your own job. Just imagine: You could have a successful business up and running before you even leave school.
- Equipped with effective communication skills, you're now ready to navigate personal and professional relationships with clarity, empathy, and understanding. Emotional intelligence will give your mental health a boost.
- From cooking and laundry to basic car maintenance, you've gained practical knowledge that will help you live on your own with confidence when the time

comes. You now have the skills that make you self-reliant and capable of running your own household.

- By prioritizing balanced eating, quality sleep, regular exercise, and stress management, you've laid the groundwork for a vibrant and fulfilling life. You can work hard to reach your goals, but you also have to take regular breaks; otherwise, you will just get burned out.
- With insights into trust, respect, boundaries, and the dynamics of romantic relationships, you're prepared to form healthy relationships. Remember that relationships are about give and take; you're not just in one to make your partner happy and fulfill all their needs. Always stand up for yourself and make sure that people respect your boundaries.
- With a good understanding of time management, responsibility, and routine-building, you're ready to embrace adulthood with maturity and confidence.

The skills you've gained aren't just tools—they're the building blocks of your future success and fulfillment. Embrace the challenges, seize the opportunities, and make the most of every moment. Enjoy your teenage years, but keep learning and striving.

Remember that you're never alone. Involve your parents in your growth journey, lean on them for support and guidance, and get the support you need to navigate the path ahead with courage and resilience.

This book is also there to guide you. Refer back to these pages when you need support.

Embrace your journey and the bright future ahead. Your potential is limitless, and you can make a valuable contribution to the world.

Glossary

Adaptability: Picture this: You're all set for a fun day at the skate park, but then it starts pouring rain. Instead of getting bummed out, you grab your board and go to the indoor skate park for a new adventure. That's adaptability—making the best of unexpected changes.

Assertiveness: Whether speaking up in class or standing your ground in a friendly game of basketball, assertiveness means confidently expressing yourself while respecting others' boundaries and opinions. It's about being clear and confident in what you want without being pushy.

Communication Skills: From chatting with your buddies about the latest online games to giving a killer presentation in class, communication skills are essential. It's not just about talking but also listening and understanding others. Remember, sometimes a nod or a smile can say more than words.

Conflict Resolution: Ever disagreed with a friend or sibling about something? Conflict resolution is all about finding a fair solution through calm discussion and compromise. It's not about who's right or wrong, but finding common ground and moving forward together.

Critical Thinking: Think of critical thinking like being a detective—analyzing clues, asking questions, and piecing together the puzzle. You have to look beyond the surface and make smart decisions based on evidence and logic.

Cyberbully: A cyberbully is someone who uses the internet or phones to hurt or scare others on purpose. They might send mean messages, share secrets without permission, or spread lies online. Cyberbullying can hurt people's feelings and make them feel bad about themselves.

Decision Making: Whether it's choosing what to have for lunch or deciding on your future career path, decision-making is a part of everyday life. It's about weighing your options, considering the consequences, and going with your gut.

Digital Literacy: In a world where social media trends come and go faster than you can say "viral," it's important to be digitally literate. You need to know how to navigate the online world safely and responsibly, from protecting your privacy to spotting fake news.

Emotional Intelligence: Do you instinctively know when others feel down? That's emotional intelligence—understanding and managing your own feelings, as well as empathizing with others. It's about being in tune with yourself and those around you.

Empathy: Imagine walking in someone else's shoes for a day—feeling what they feel and seeing the world through their eyes. That's empathy—caring about others' experiences and showing kindness and understanding, even when you don't agree with them. However, never compromise on your values for others, even when you understand how they feel.

Etiquette and Manners: Knowing when to say "please" and "thank you" or how to set the table at dinner shows respect and consideration for others. It's all about being polite in any situation.

Financial Literacy: Understanding basic money concepts from a young age is important. Budgeting your allowance, saving for something you want, and knowing the difference between needs and wants are all part of financial literacy.

Flapper: A flapper is a rubber valve that controls the flow of water from the toilet tank to the bowl. This simple mechanism helps regulate the flushing process and ensures that water is released efficiently to clean the bowl.

Goal Setting: Whether it's mastering a new skate trick or acing that math test, setting goals gives you something to strive for. It's about breaking big dreams into smaller, achievable steps and celebrating each victory along the way.

Healthy Relationships: Friends who've got your back, family who support you, and maybe even a special someone who makes your heart skip a beat—healthy relationships are the foundation of a happy life. It's about mutual respect, trust, and open communication.

Leadership Skills: Whether you're rallying your friends for a pickup game or taking charge of a group project, leadership is about inspiring others to work together towards a common goal. It's not just about being the loudest voice but also being the one who listens and guides others.

Online Communication: This can include texting, chatting on social media platforms like Instagram or Snapchat, sending emails, participating in online forums or discussion groups, or even video chatting through apps like Zoom or FaceTime. It's a cool way to keep in touch with your family or friends, wherever they are in the world.

Peer Pressure: This term refers to the influence exerted by one's peers or social group. They want you to behave in certain ways or make certain choices to fit in or gain acceptance from the group. Confident people are less likely to become victims of peer pressure.

Personal Hygiene: Okay, let's get real—no one wants to hang out with the guy who hasn't showered in a week. Personal hygiene is about taking care of yourself, from brushing your teeth to washing your hands regularly. It's not just about looking good but feeling good, too.

Problem-Solving: Ever been stumped by a tricky math problem or locked out of your house with no spare key? Problem-solving is all about finding creative solutions to life's challenges, whether big or small. It's about staying calm, thinking outside the box, and never giving up.

Resilience: Life can throw some curveballs your way, from failing a test to getting your heart broken. Resilience is about bouncing back from setbacks, learning from your mistakes, and coming back even stronger. Be like a rubber band—flexible and tough to break.

Self-Care: Taking care of yourself is about making time for things that make you happy, whether it's shooting hoops with friends or listening to your favorite music. Remember, you can't take care of everything in your life, as you'll burn out if you never take a break.

Self-Confidence: It's that feeling of believing in yourself and your abilities, even when things get tough. It's about knowing you've got what it takes to tackle whatever life throws your way.

Side Hustle: A side hustle is a part-time job, gig, or project outside your regular schoolwork or commitments to earn extra money or explore your interests. It could involve anything from tutoring, pet sitting, or babysitting. Some young people even offer freelance services like graphic design or writing. Side hustles can help you gain valuable skills, experience, and independence while you pursue your interests and gain some money.

SMART Goals: These are specific, measurable, achievable, relevant, and time-bound objectives designed to provide clear direction and motivation.

Stress Management: This involves techniques and strategies you can use to cope with and reduce feelings of stress, anxiety, and pressure in your daily life. You need to identify your stressors, practice relaxation techniques such as deep breathing or mindfulness, set realistic goals and priorities, maintain a healthy lifestyle with regular exercise and proper nutrition, and find support from adults when needed.

Time Management: With school, sports, hobbies, and maybe even a part-time job, life can feel like a juggling act. Time management is about organizing your schedule, prioritizing tasks, and making the most of every minute. It's about finding balance and making time for the most important things.

Toxic Relationship: This type of relationship is characterized by unhealthy behavior, communication, and interaction between people that are bad for emotional well-being, self-esteem, and overall mental health. Toxic relationships often involve manipulation, control, emotional abuse, or other forms of harmful behavior that could cause people to feel stressed, anxious, and unhappy.

REFERENCES

Adams, R. *(2023,* October 05*) 30 best side hustles for teens*. (2023). Nasdaq. https://www.nasdaq.com/articles/30-best-side-hustles-for-teens-in-person-online-2023

Alvord, M., & Halfond, R. (2019, October 24). *How to help children and teens manage their stress*. American Psychological Association. https://www.apa.org/topics/children/stress

American Academy of Pediatrics. (2019). *What's going on in the teenage brain?* HealthyChildren.org. https://www.healthychildren.org/English/ages-stages/teen/Pages/Whats-Going-On-in-the-Teenage-Brain.aspx

Barendse, M. E. A., Cheng, T. W., & Pfeifer, J. H. (2020). *Your brain on puberty*. Frontiers for Young Minds, https://doi.org/10.3389/frym.2020.00053

Beecher, K. *(*May 2, 2022). *Help your teen get more exercise*. Mayo Clinic Health System. https://www.mayoclinichealthsystem.org/hometown-health/speaking-of-health/teens-and-exercise#:~:text=It%20releases%20stress%2Dbusting%20endorphins

Boys & Girls Clubs of America. (2022, January 19). *The importance of goal-setting for teens*. BGCA. https://www.bgca.org/news-stories/2022/January/the-importance-of-goal-setting-for-teens

Brin, C. (2023, May 22, 2023). *Ultimate guide to budgeting for young adults & teens*. Hyperjar. https://hyperjar.com/blog/money-management-ultimate-guide-to-budgeting-for-young-adults-and-teens

Care.com. (2023, August 21). *10 expert-backed time management tips for teenagers and kids starting secondary school*. Care.com. https://www.care.com/c/en-gb/time-management-tips-for-teenagers-and-kids/

Communication Skills World. (2017, August 22). *Importance of communication skills for teenagers*. Communication Skills World. https://www.communicationskillsworld.com/communicationskillsforteens.html

Dellaquila, D. (2022, November 16). *How to help teens with conflict resolution*. Gateway to Solutions. https://www.gatewaytosolutions.org/how-to-help-teens-with-conflict-resolution

(2021, March 17). *What are taxes? A super simple explanation for kids, teens, and beginners*. Easy Peasy Finance for Kids and Beginners.

https://www.easypeasyfinance.com/taxes-for-kids-teens-beginners/

Engler, B. *(2022,* September 2). *Building conflict resolution skills in children*. (n.d.). Connections Academy. https://www.connectionsacademy.com/support/resources/article/building-conflict-resolution-skills-in-children

Exercise for teenagers: How much they need, and how to fit it In. (2022, April 13). Healthline. https://www.healthline.com/health/fitness/exercise-for-teenagers#questions-to-ask

Flatley, K. (2022, September 20). *Teach kids how to be savvy with their money*. Self-Sufficient Kids. https://selfsufficientkids.com/teach-kids-comparison-shop/

Garey, J. (2016, January 29). *How to help teenagers get more sleep*. Child Mind Institute. https://childmind.org/article/help-teenagers-get-sleep/

Gavin, M. (n.d.). *5 Ideas for better sleep (for teens)*.KidsHealth. https://kidshealth.org/en/teens/tips-sleep.html

Exercise for teenagers: How much they need, and how to fit it In. (2022, April 13). Healthline. https://www.healthline.com/health/fitness/exercise-for-teenagers#questions-to-ask

Health Direct. (2019, September 27). *Puberty for boys*. Healthdirect Australia. https://www.healthdirect.gov.au/puberty-for-boys

How to learn basic laundry skills before college. (2014, June 5). Your Teen Magazine. https://yourteenmag.com/teens-college/college-life/how-to-do-laundry

Introduction to relationships. (2016, April 19). Teen Health Source. https://teenhealthsource.com/relationships/introduction-relationships/

Jacobson, R. (n.d.).*Teaching kids about boundaries*. Child Mind Institute. https://childmind.org/article/teaching-kids-boundaries-empathy/#rules-work-both-ways

Kelly, A. (2019, January 16). *Take charge of your health: A guide for teenagers*. National Institute of Diabetes and Digestive and Kidney Diseases. https://www.niddk.nih.gov/health-information/weight-management/take-charge-health-guide-teenagers

Kidshealth *(2014). Boys and puberty (for kids).* KidsHealth. https://kidshealth.org/en/kids/boys-puberty.html

KidsHealth Behavioral Health Experts. (n.d.). *Peer pressure (for teens)*. KidsHealth.

https://kidshealth.org/en/teens/peer-pressure.html?ref=search

Leopold, B. (n.d.). *How to explain respect to a teenager*. Overcomers Counseling. https://overcomewithus.com/parenting/how-to-explain-respect-to-a-teenager

Lyness, D. (2022, February). *Dealing with peer pressure (for kids)*. KidsHealth. https://kidshealth.org/en/kids/peer-pressure.html

Mydoh. *(2022, July 20). Emergency funds explained for teens*. Mydoh. https://www.mydoh.ca/learn/money-101/building-credit/emergency-funds-explained-for-teens/

Paris, D. (2022, March 7). *Debt 101: A guide for parents and teenagers*. Mydoh. https://www.mydoh.ca/learn/money-101/debt/debt-101-a-guide-for-parents-and-teenagers/

Pearl, E. (2018). *Online safety (for teens)*. KidsHealth. https://kidshealth.org/en/teens/internet-safety.html

Psych Central. (2014, September 27). *5 tips to help you adapt to change*. Psych Central. https://psychcentral.com/blog/adapting-to-change#why-its-hard

(n.d.). *Relationships and romance: Pre-teens and teenagers*. Raising Children Network. https://raisingchildren.net.au/pre-teens/communicating-relationships/romantic-relationships/teen-relationships#:~:text=Teenage%20romance%20and%20relationships%20are

Salamon, K. (n.d.). *Mindfulness (for teens)*. KidsHealth. https://kidshealth.org/en/teens/mindfulness.html

Selby. (2023, August 24). *Nonverbal communication skills for high schoolers: A visual guide*. Everyday Speech. https://everydayspeech.com/sel-implementation/nonverbal-communication-skills-for-high-schoolers-a-visual-guide-2/

Van Duzer, T. (2020, October 23). *Time management techniques for teens: The Ultimate Guide*. Student-Tutor Education Blog. https://student-tutor.com/blog/time-management-techniques-for-teens/

*Wills, J. (*June 12, 2023*). Successful teens know how to prioritize.* Psychology Today. https://www.psychologytoday.com/gb/blog/radical-teaching/202305/successful-teens-know-how-to-prioritize

Printed in Great Britain
by Amazon

48482051R00086